HAUNTED HELENA

MONTANA'S QUEEN CITY GHOSTS

ELLEN BAUMLER

Haunted America

Published by Haunted America
A Division of The History Press
Charleston, SC 29403
www.historypress.net

All cover images courtesy of Chloe Katsilas, Rio de Luz Photography.

First published 2014

Manufactured in the United States

ISBN 978.1.60949.934.1

Library of Congress CIP data applied for.

CONTENTS

ACKNOWLEDGEMENTS

Writing a book is a journey, and there are always U-turns and detours. *Haunted Helena* has been no exception. Many friends, colleagues and acquaintances have helped me along the way, offered encouragement and contributed to these pages. I appreciate each of them.

I especially thank those who came forward to share their experiences with me and then allowed me to retell them. I hope readers will appreciate that it is not always easy to share incidents and events that are personal. There would be no *Haunted Helena* without your stories.

Thanks to my daughter, Katie Baumler-Morales, who carefully read every draft—more than once—and offered excellent critiques. Jon Axline and Charleen Spalding also offered careful critiques of some of the chapters.

Chloe Katsilas of Rio de Luz Photography generously donated her time, freely offered her photography skills, lugged her camera around to numerous places and took many of the photos that appear on these pages.

Finally, thanks to my husband, Mark, for his tolerance and patience over many nights and weekends at the computer and for allowing me to tell our family's story.

Introduction

IT BEGINS AT HOME

A heavy spring snowfall spread like a blanket over Helena on Easter Monday 1988. Our tiny cabin at the Lamplighter Motel was warm and cozy. My husband, Mark; our three-year-old daughter, Katie; two cats; and a cocker spaniel had made the long trip from Tucson. We felt like pioneers heading into unknown territory. Montana was to be our new home.

The April snow made tiny streams and rivulets in its rapid melt as we began our frantic search for housing. Mark was soon to start his new job as state archaeologist, the moving van was three days behind us and we were desperate. We looked at everything on the market, but nothing seemed right. Bill Spilker, our congenial realtor, shrugged in frustration.

"Isn't there anything else you can show us?"

"Well," Bill said, "there is one more. But I think it's too big for three of you. Still, we can take a look."

The two-story, Italianate-style house sat on a busy corner at Eleventh Avenue and Raleigh Street. My heart skipped a beat as we climbed the steps to the front porch. Bill turned the key in the lock. We stepped across the threshold, and we knew that we had come home. The house, built in 1888, had just hit the century mark. It needed work, but it had beautiful high ceilings, a spacious kitchen and great potential. Plus, it was empty and ready (or waiting?) for us. We moved in a couple days later.

That first night, I awakened to radio static. I reached over to turn off my clock radio, but it wasn't on. I got up to search for the sound. I could hear faint threads of music and something like conversation over the static, but

The historic Wick-Seiler Residence has been home to the Baumler family since 1988.
Ellen Baumler.

the sounds were too low to identify. I went back to bed annoyed and listened to the radio for a long time. I finally drifted back to sleep and forgot about it.

The second night, the same thing happened. I awakened as before to the sound of the radio. Again, through the static I heard music and voices. A search of the upstairs turned up no radio. I said nothing until it happened a third time. I told Mark that something was keeping me awake at night. His expression was odd. "Have you heard the radio, too?" he asked.

We accepted the radio as an odd quirk, and from time to time, we heard it in the night. It never made us uncomfortable; it was just annoying. Turmoil in the household seemed to bring it on. If one of us was sick, if we had troubles or if the furniture was displaced during our endless renovations, we would likely hear it. Sometimes it visited only one of us; other times, we all heard it at the same time.

Katie chose the bedroom at the top of the stairs, and we settled in. We had not been in the house long when one morning at breakfast she announced that footsteps on the stairs had awakened her. She was not afraid; rather she said matter-of-factly, "That was John coming home last night." We had

8

no idea who John was or where Katie came up with the name, but as we began to research the home's past, that piece seemed to fit. John Wick, an early owner, was a prominent saloonkeeper and would have kept late hours. I realize now that children are sometimes more sensitive than adults to residual energy.

Katie never slept well in that room, and night terrors regularly plagued her. When she tried to articulate what was scaring her, she could only identify the window as the source of her dread. We moved her to the other bedroom, and sometime later, a former resident knocked on our door. We invited her in and showed her around. When we got to the room at the top of the stairs, she commented offhand that her daughter was about Katie's age and this had been her room. "Strange," she said. "My daughter never slept well in this room. She was terrified of the window."

We became acquainted with John Wick's grandchildren, Art Seiler Jr. and Bernice Seiler Mitchell. The delightful brother and sister, both well into their eighties when we first met them, grew up in our house and had very fond memories. They visited us several times, sharing family history and childhood adventures. Their grandfather John purchased the house and the cottage next door on Raleigh Street in 1898. He and his wife, Mina, had three children. In 1901, their daughter, Elizabeth, married Arthur Seiler Sr. in a ceremony in our living room bay. It was Elizabeth's twentieth birthday.

John and Mina Wick, like their son-in-law, were German immigrants, and the family spoke their native language at home. Seiler became the longtime editor of Helena's German language newspaper. He came to the United States in 1889 at fifteen on the ship *Westernland*. He spoke no English and traveled alone. When he finally arrived at Helena via the Northern Pacific, he was to work for an uncle. His uncle, however, had disappeared. The German community took Seiler in. He learned English, apprenticed under candy maker Frank Hepperdiezal and learned the trade. Until he died in 1968, Seiler grieved because he thought his uncle had abandoned him. Family members later discovered, however, that prior to Seiler's arrival in Helena, the uncle had been traveling along a remote trail on business when he was ambushed and murdered.

John Wick passed away in 1908. Although he helped lay the cornerstone of the German Lutheran Church on nearby Rodney Street, the funeral took place at home as was the custom. After Wick's death, Arthur and Elizabeth moved into the family home with their two small children, newborn Art Jr. and six-year-old Bernice.

Arthur Seiler, Sr., (center) with his German band, maintained his German roots. *Leslee Coleman.*

In the early 1930s, the Seilers converted the upstairs to an apartment for Bernice and her husband, Harry M. Mitchell. The house passed out of the Seiler family in 1957. Art Jr. and Bernice delighted in visiting their childhood home, and we always let them tour the house. Art was tall and straight; Bernice was very tiny, maybe four feet, nine inches, and quite a character. She drove a huge Cadillac until she was ninety-eight. On one visit, when they were both quite elderly, we slowly climbed the stairs. When we got to room at the top, Art turned to me and said, "You know, back in the 1910s, I had Helena's first radio operation set up in here. It took up the entire room, and people came from all over town just to hear my radio." I knew immediately that this explained our ghostly radio.

"Art," I asked, "did you get good reception on that radio?"

"Oh," he answered, "the reception was terrible. There was static all the time."

I hesitated to tell Art about our radio. He was Montana's first graduate of MIT, an award-winning businessman, an inventor/designer of numerous industrial improvements, an experienced pilot and a World War II veteran, and he loved technology. I gathered up my courage and said, "Art, you know, sometimes we hear a radio in the night."

He chuckled, "Well. How about that? I am not surprised. We played that darn radio so much, its energy probably absorbed into the walls."

The experience taught me that people, animals and even electrical appliances expend energy. Where does it go when the source is no longer there or turned off? Energy can remain long after the source is gone, and sometimes it resurfaces, or replays, almost like a time warp. That explains our radio. But I don't want to take that too far. Some years after we figured out the radio, a person sensitive to this kind of energy said to me, "Maybe the radio is meant to protect you. Next time you hear it, try to discover what is underneath it. Maybe it's there to keep you from hearing something else." I prefer not to think about that.

The radio is not the only window to the past in our house. The past has left us little gifts, small things that might seem coincidental. But for those of us who love old places and whose lives intertwine with the past, coincidences make perfect sense. The power of the past lives in these comfortable old homes, and it rewards us for our reverence with subtle glimpses of its former occupants. These glimpses teach us to respect the "power of place."

One morning, I was home alone and had vacuumed the den. I briefly stepped out of the room and returned to find a very old marble sitting in the center of the floor. Where did it come from? It was weird, but I loved this little gift. As time went on, other marbles turned up—on the stairway after I had vacuumed, on the basement floor, in the heating returns, in the garden and, recently, one washed out of the drain spout after a storm. Each is unique, from different time periods. I keep them in a special box, so they remain connected to the place where they were found. I am not alone in finding these little gifts. Many people over the years have shared their own discoveries with me. I call them "spirit tailings." Like the dirt that miners sifted through and cast aside into tailing piles, these "tailings" serve a special purpose. Whether you find marbles, pennies, buttons or other things—these little gifts serve to remind us that the past is always with us.

There were other things, too. The house needed work, and for three years, I stripped endless layers of wallpaper and painted the worn woodwork. Sometimes as I worked, I felt a tap on my shoulder. I clearly recall brushing at my right shoulder, always the right one. I never thought much about it, but I was conscious enough of this peculiar phenomenon to be aware of it a number of times.

The Baumlers' home has yielded up marbles of different vintages. *Ellen Baumler.*

Some years later, a friend of Katie's was visiting, and her mom came to the house to pick her up. I had never met the woman. I invited her in, and she admired the house and asked for a tour. We came to the room at the top of the stairs—Katie's former bedroom and the room where Art had his radio. She stepped in and suddenly clutched her chest.

"The air is heavy in here, and I can't breathe," she gasped as she stepped back into the hall. I confess that I was horrified.

I showed her the rest of the house, and when we came to the den, located directly below the radio bedroom, she had the same scary reaction as upstairs and said that she could not breathe in the room. It was odd. As she left with her daughter, she said to me, "I have never been in a real haunted house, but yours is definitely haunted. I have to ask if you have ever felt a tap on your shoulder."

I don't know why she asked that question. I had never been frightened of anything in my house before, nor have any of my experiences in places across the state affected me in this way. But that one time, at that moment, my blood ran cold, and I was truly afraid.

An explanation for the breathing difficulty came soon after. The last time Art visited us, he told me that our den was originally his parents' bedroom. He recalled that his mother had an unreasonable fear of thunderstorms, and she would take him into the closet in that room. The closet is tucked under the stairway. I opened the small door, and Art peered in at the books and toys we stored there. I saw him shiver. He told me that he and his mother would huddle there in complete darkness until the storm passed. He would first be pressed into the heavy clothing that was stuffed into that closet. He couldn't breathe and felt that he would suffocate. Apparently, Art's negative childhood energy lingers in that part of the house.

After my dad died in July 2000, I acquired a wonderful antique oak hall tree. I put it in the kitchen and hung my dad's cowboy hat on one hook and my mom's on the other. One day, I came home from work to find Katie, who was by then in middle school, sitting at the kitchen table pale and shaken. She pointed to the floor, and there was my mom's cowboy hat. Katie said it whizzed past her, flew across the table and landed on the opposite side of the room. This was the first of half a dozen times that my mom's hat flew off the hall tree.

One evening, we were in the den watching TV and heard our two dogs growling. The dogs never growled. We found them circling the hat, which was again on the floor on the other side of the kitchen. Another time, I was standing next to the hall tree when the hat flew past my head. I always took the flying hat to be a message from my dad that I needed to check in with my mom. In retrospect, although she seemed fine, I now realize that my mom was fighting the dementia that has taken her memory. I think my dad was trying to tell me that she was not well.

In the first minutes of September 11, 2001, before the terrorist attack on the New York Trade Center, Mark and I had an unsettling experience. As I came through the living room on my way up to bed just after midnight, something on the wall between the picture molding and the ceiling caught my eye. It was big and very black. I thought it was a spider, but it was way too large. As I looked at it, it moved. I felt a chill. Suddenly the thing unfolded itself and left the wall in a swoop. I let out a short scream. Then I realized it was a very large bat.

We threw open the door. The bat circled around and around the dining room and finally flew out. We had never seen bats near the house nor have we since. The next morning, as the nation watched in horror, it became clear that 9/11 would forever be etched in our memories. Oddly enough, my mother was born on September 11, 1922, and John Wick died on September 11, 1908. These odd connections are too bizarre to be purely coincidental.

Bernice Mitchell passed away in 2003, two days short of her 101st birthday. Art preceded his sister, passing away at 94 on December 26, 2002. The week of Art's death, our computer went berserk. After replacing every possible component to no avail, the company gave us a new computer. As the repairman left after the last three or four house calls, he recommended that we call an electrician and have the wiring checked. So we did. The electrician found that the plug was not grounded and could have sparked, causing a fire. Given Art's love for technology, his keen knowledge of electrical things and his fondness for our house, we are certain that he was warning us.

We converted the fourth upstairs bedroom, formerly Bernice Mitchell's kitchen, into a large bathroom in 2011. During the renovation, the contractor told me when he was upstairs and alone in the house, he heard something like small objects tossed down the hallway. He said he thought they sounded like marbles. Bernice—an avid golfer who made her first hole in one at eighty-two—told me that her husband used to practice golf shots upstairs. He broke the light fixture many times, but he owned a furniture store and could always get replacement glass. Maybe the contractor heard golf balls bouncing down the hall.

I have often imagined Bernice cooking in her kitchen. Sometimes, we have awakened in the wee hours to the smell of bacon frying or coffee brewing. On our first Thanksgiving in the house, we all noticed the rich smell of roasting turkey that wafted through the upstairs before we put our own bird in the oven. Bernice was so tiny that she always wore shoes with heels. On one occasion, footsteps in the night awakened me. It sounded like a woman in heels. The sound was weirdly hollow. I couldn't tell exactly where it came from, but it echoed eerily in the dark.

And there have been many other things, too. During kitchen renovations, Katie heard ghostly knocking inside the stove; the dogs heard it as well. And the spray nozzle in the sink suddenly came on when the water was turned off. Katie's stereo had a mind of its own. It would suddenly turn on, blaring, frightening her and her friends. Our friend Jon Axline twice came in to feed the fish when we were out of town to find the cowboy hat on the floor, and once while in the kitchen, he heard footsteps overhead on the roof. I have heard them, too. Another time, Jon's daughter Kate came in to feed the fish while we were away. She was in the kitchen when she heard deliberate footsteps, like someone in men's dress shoes, walking across the living room. She fled!

Mark is the resident skeptic. He can't deny the events we all have experienced, but he is not ready to say he believes in ghosts. However, on Mondays, when he gets home before I do, he waters the plants. Heading up the stairs with the house empty and quiet, he says he sometimes feels a presence up there, waiting for him. His habit is to announce himself. "It's just me, coming up to water the plants," he calls out, just in case.

In October 2012, I lost a necklace that I cherished. It was a heavy, wide silver band that had belonged to my mother. I wore it often and missed it about two weeks before Halloween. After looking everywhere, I gave up. I had recently bought a little antique shelf with cubbyholes that I had put on my bedroom dresser. Days later as I took down the pictures and knickknacks to dust, there on the top shelf was my necklace, neatly laid out in a perfect semi-circle. Mark didn't put it there, nor did I. I thanked the house for returning it.

The radio had long been silent. At the end of that Halloween week 2012, I was already up and downstairs early one morning. We were agonizing over

Katie—who had been living far away in New Zealand since January—and whether or not she would make the long trip home for Christmas. Mark had awakened before his alarm and lay there anticipating it. Those early morning hours, with the house very still, were always a common time to hear the ghostly radio. And this morning, conditions apparently were right. He heard the faint static and low conversation familiar from all those times before. It seemed to be letting him know that our resident spirits—or whatever they are—had not gone anywhere. That year, 2012, the house left us no "spirit tailings" for Christmas, but Katie did make it home for the holidays. I think the house was as happy as we were.

The next year, Katie and Sergio, her fiancé, came home at Christmas to be married. The wedding was small and lovely in our living room bay window, where Elizabeth Wick and Art Seiler Sr. were married so long ago. Both Mark and I heard the radio in the weeks leading up to the wedding. I anticipated some activity, but there was none. I know the house was excited, though; I could feel it. The week before the wedding, in the middle of the night, I heard two crashes. The dog growled, and I leapt out of bed. Mark heard it, too. I flipped the light switch and found that my Vera Bradley overnight suitcase had somehow fallen off the closet's top shelf. My travel dryer had been in the bag, but it somehow fell out—which explains the first loud crash. The suitcase, however, landed right side up. The quilted cloth bag could hardly have made a second crash.

The wedding was perfect, and the house looked beautiful. The four of us—Katie, Sergio, Mark and I—traveled to Puerto Rico for New Year's to meet our new son-in-law's family. The trip was wonderful but uneventful, and Jon Axline looked after the house. He reported nothing odd.

This just proves my theory that you can't anticipate supernatural activity. It never happens when you think it will, or when you want it to.

Chapter 1

SHADOWS OF THE GOLD CAMP

The gold in the gravel of Last Chance Gulch fueled financial empires and built Montana's capital city. The legacy of the gold rush lives on in Helena's flamboyant architecture and luxurious West Side homes that dazzle visitors today. But Helena is also a place of secrets, nestled in its crooked bed along the famous gulch. Besides a colorful history, Helena has a clandestine past of layered energy, where shadows lurk in darkened doorways, intense emotions linger and roaming spirits leave no footprints.

Tribal histories and archaeology tell us that generations of Native Americans trekked through the game-rich Helena valley, planting the first layer of energy. Early people knew the valley as a place where earthquakes made the ground tremble. They left their handprints and mysterious paintings on nearby cliff walls and their stone tools and projectile points scattered across the valley. Members of the Lewis and Clark expedition also traveled through, noting in their journals the Gates of the Rocky Mountains.

Antelope, rattlesnakes and grizzly bears were plentiful when four prospectors happened upon the gulch on July 14, 1864. Known to posterity as the Four Georgians for the placer mining method they practiced, the down-on-their-luck foursome was en route to Virginia City for supplies. They decided to give it one more try, dug holes and crouched along the banks of the clear stream with their gold pans, swishing and swirling water and gravel. Their discovery touched off changes to the valley.

Miners churned up the wilderness and stripped the forests. By 1869, Last Chance Gulch had given up nearly $18 million worth of the golden treasure,

A.E. Matthews sketched an early panorama of Helena, published in 1868. *MHS Research Center.*

and the gulch looked nothing like it had a few years previous. But log cabins built close together were vulnerable to the fires that haunted early residents. Their survival depended on goods freighted far distances. If fire claimed their food supply, there was no immediate replacement. And this anxiety provided a third kind of energy. Early businessmen were in such a hurry to build fireproof stores and offices that brick and stone buildings covered the diggings before the gold had entirely played out. Legend has it that as late as 1913, excavation for the Placer Hotel yielded enough gold to pay for the building and then some. Helena is literally built on gold.

In the earliest days of the gold camp, miners worked at a feverish pitch. At the south end of Last Chance Gulch, where it divides into Grizzly and Oro Fino Gulches, a prospector from California built a cabin. The log dwelling served as the entrance to his claim, and he worked it, digging (or "drifting") into the hillside. He was an older man who kept to himself, and perhaps that is why there was talk about him. Some believed that he was a murderer and a fugitive. There was something else about this miner. He had the Midas touch. Every bucket of rock he dug yielded gold. Everyone knew he had amassed a huge hoard that he stored in his drift, and some were jealous.

Then one night the miner disappeared. He wasn't exactly missed, as no one cared where he had gone, but it was strange that he wasn't around anymore. What he had in his drift was common knowledge, and many a miner cast his gaze longingly toward the old man's cabin. Late one night, two men took courage and "jumped" the old man's claim. They entered the cabin and spread out their bedrolls, thinking that they would investigate the drift in the morning. They settled into sleep. Suddenly, both men jolted awake.

The back of the cabin led into the old man's diggings, and from the tunnel came an unearthly white-bright light that spilled out into the cabin and filled it with a strange glow. This light was weird and frightening. Then came a blood-curdling, piercing scream of agony, and at the mine's threshold, surrounded by the bright light, were two men locked in a death grip, one on top of the other. As the old miner struggled with all his might, the man on top raised his arm. In his hand, he held a dagger that glinted as it caught the light. Thus poised, for a fleeting moment, the light revealed his face—a friend known to the two claim jumpers. Down came his arm in a rapid movement as the knife pierced the old man's heart. In a flash, the vision was over, and the cabin was again enveloped in darkness. The two men fled the cabin and slept no more that night.

The next day, they told their tale and identified the man they had seen wielding the dagger. But suspicion had already begun to take hold, and this added credence to the conclusion others had already drawn. A search revealed the old miner's cold, stiff body far back in the drift, with the savage, gaping wound that took his life. The gold he had worked so hard to find was missing.

The Helena *Daily Independent* recounted this story some years after the fact on November 28, 1875, speculating that in some eerie coincidence, the two claim jumpers had the same dream. The paper does not bring up the other possibility: that the claim jumpers actually saw the apparition. Did the energy of the miner's last desperate moments and the thief's murderous rage cause the unholy event to play again in front of the claim jumpers? Either way, it solved the mystery of the miner's disappearance.

Longtime Helena resident Gus Beaver, who passed away at ninety-three in 2004, lived most of his life at the south end of Last Chance Gulch. He knew all the lore of the neighborhood. In an interview in 1996, Gus claimed that Chinese miners working underground in the nearby hills were murdered when white miners blasted the entry to their tunnel, sealing them inside. Gus believed their spirits were restless. He told a homeowner whose property was on that site not to locate her children's bedroom in the daylight basement. "Because," said Gus, "the children might be awakened by those dead miners

Miners in gum boots panned streams across Montana looking for gold. "The Prospector," sketch for the *Helena Board of Trade, 1887.*

scratching on their windows." While no record of such disaster has come to light, there may be a thread of truth to the story. Perhaps the spirit of that other old miner wanders the south end of the gulch, searching for the gold that went missing when he gave up his life in the drift.

When the Four Georgians made their discovery, the territory of Montana, created on May 26, 1864, was less than two months old. Carved from the huge Idaho Territory, Congress created Montana to bring more accessible government and law enforcement to the remote mining camps. The Montana gold camps suffered because the capital of Idaho Territory and the seat of government were in Lewiston, Idaho, miles across the rugged, sometimes impassable Continental Divide. The gold rushes brought unsavory characters and a dangerous criminal element. With no law enforcement or government presence, the miners' courts, patterned after those in California, were ill equipped to handle the vicious crimes that threatened Montana's early settlements.

Law enforcement was slow in coming. Vigilantes took the law into their own hands to rid the new, booming settlements of this criminal element.

Their actions are still controversial. In the space of several months in late 1863 and early 1864, vigilantes hanged some two dozen men at Bannack and Virginia City. A splinter group operated in Helena, where the infamous Hangman's Tree saw ten named victims and several other unknown men hanged on its limbs between 1865 and 1870.

The Murderer's Tree, as it was first known, stood east of the settlement at the head of Dry Gulch, between present-day Highland and Hillsdale Streets, just west of Blake Street. The ancient Ponderosa pine, according to those who knew it well, had massive lower branches that tangled in weird, fantastic contortions. The branches, bleak and devoid of foliage, protruded some twenty feet from its gnarled, moss-covered trunk. Miners, even in their need to cut logs for cabins and sluices, let it stand, looming over the eastern outskirts of the gold camp.

Violence in Montana's mining camps affected everyone, and the Murderer's Tree quickly became a community icon. Twelve-year-old Mary "Mollie" Sheehan, later Mrs. Peter Ronan, recalled in her memoir, *Girl from the Gulches*, that one morning in 1865 or 1866, as she and her classmates reached the crest of the Broadway hill on their way to school, they saw a man hanging from the tree. He stayed there for three days as a warning, and the boys flocked to view the "bad man" at every opportunity. Mollie hated the talk and recalled "that pitiful object, with bruised head, disarrayed vest and trousers, with boots so stiff, so worn, so wrinkled, so strangely the most poignant of all the gruesome details." All her life she tried to forget, but nearly seventy years later, as she dictated her memories to her daughter, Mary still remembered.

David Hilger, who came to Helena as a youngster with his family in 1867, recalled climbing the tree's dead branches and examining rope burns on its lower limbs. He and his friends played marbles beneath it. On April 30, 1870, their game was interrupted for the lynchings of Arthur Compton and Joseph Wilson. The two were being held in the county jail when citizens forced it open, took the two to the steps of the courthouse and conducted an open-air trial in protest of the fledgling, slow-to-act government. The "jury" found them guilty of the robbery and attempted murder of a local rancher. The crowd voted to hang the two and marched them to the accepted place of execution, by this time known as the Hangman's Tree. Once the double hanging was over, according to Hilger, the boys resumed their game. These were the last two recorded hangings on the Hangman's Tree.

In 1875, Reverend W.E. Shippen paid a woodcutter $2.50 to chop the Hangman's Tree into firewood. He claimed that flooding loosened the roots

A.E Matthews sketched Helena's Hangman's Tree in 1865. *MHS Research Center*.

of the dead tree and that it was in danger of toppling onto his barn and killing his horse. He did not anticipate the public outcry at the removal of the tree. Citizens lined up by the hundreds to cut souvenir slivers from its trunk. Years later, in 1913, workers digging a foundation hit roots of the tree and discovered that there was no flood damage; the roots were still secure. The reverend likely made up an excuse to remove the macabre symbol.

Records show that several of the tree's victims were buried in various cemeteries, but the burial places of others are unknown. At least two coffins have surfaced in the neighborhood where the Hangman's Tree once stood. In 1900, a workman digging a foundation for an addition in a backyard uncovered one coffin. A crew hit the other working on gas lines on Davis Street in 1931. Were these victims of the Hangman's Tree? Both burials were close to the spot where the tree once stood.

David Hilger, who witnessed that last double hanging, examined the contents of the pine box discovered in 1931. According to newspaper accounts, a few shreds of clothing included the remains of the victim's boots. Hilger compared the boots, which were high-topped and had ornamental stitching, with a photograph of the hanging of James Daniels, which took place in 1866. The boots seemed to match those in the photograph. They were further described as "wrinkled." If the remains were those of Daniels, this could be the hanging Mary Ronan recalled and described.

The vigilante mentality and violent beginnings leave their marks on any community that springs from these kinds of roots. There is a fascination with the details, like Mary Ronan's recollection of wrinkled boots. A grisly photograph of the Compton and Wilson hangings in fact subdued generations of children. That photograph hung in the hallway of Jefferson Elementary School for many years, presumably as a warning that crime does not pay. And in the neighborhood where all these hangings took place, emotions must loiter in the soil, in the buildings, in the very air. Imagine the last painful gasps of all those men whose lives were snuffed out in such a violent manner. How could any of them rest in peace?

Pathways became more defined, and the neighborhood grew around the Shippen home, although the reverend was long gone. By the mid-1880s, a first generation of residents had settled there. And they and others who came after felt the energy that sometimes hung thick in the air. Even today, residents sometimes hear voices outside in the night, footsteps in their attics, and one family claims to have seen menacing apparitions in their bedroom.

Architect Herb Dawson, whose home was on Hillsdale, had a number of experiences in his house. Most frightening was an episode that occurred

The hanging of James Daniels on March 2, 1866, was one of many on the infamous Hangman's Tree. *MHS Photograph Archives.*

late one night as he was stripping paint from the parlor woodwork. A knife on the mantle behind him flew across the room and hit the wall inches from his head. Herb also found many marbles throughout his house and on the front porch.

During the remodeling of another house, workmen had applied new drywall and plaster. They locked the house and left the walls to dry. No one had access to the house, and no cats or other animals were inside. When the workmen returned, they found claw-like scratches marring every wall, and the plaster had to be reapplied. Residents find marbles, too, scattered among their homes and gardens, like those Hilger and his friends left beneath the infamous tree.

Whether you believe in the lingering energy expended in this neighborhood, not just of the victims but also of those who participated in the hangings, the neighborhood does have a unique ambience. And it began soon after the final victims took their last breaths.

On a night in the dim past, when the Hangman's Tree still stood sentinel over the barren landscape and the memories of all those terrible deaths were very fresh, a citizen had a ghoulish encounter. He detailed the incident in a letter to the editor published in the *Rocky Mountain Gazette* on September 29, 1872. He wrote that business had detained him late into the evening. It was a Saturday night and clouds heavy with snow hung low overhead. He was anxious to get home to his family and the comfort of a warm room. As he walked rapidly down Rodney Street, he felt the most peculiar compulsion to change directions. Unable to resist the strange pull, he abruptly turned east, away from his destination, and headed toward the Hangman's Tree. His eyes adjusted to the darkness as he left the small puddles of light cast by homes along the street. He could easily see the tree's stark and lifeless outline, its limbs outstretched.

When he was about twenty paces from the tree, he saw the form of a man. It appeared to be hanging a few feet below a lower limb. So startled was he that he momentarily lost his composure and had the horrific thought that vigilantes had been at their work again. He regained control of his emotions and approached the tree to discover what criminal had met his end there. The figure was dressed in dark clothing, and his back was turned. A dog's frantic barking from a distant house broke the silence, and a light wind riffled the tree's dead branches. It became clear that where there should have been a rope extending from the limb, there was none. The figure was simply suspended in midair, and it was not a solid person but rather delicately transparent.

Suddenly the figure raised its arms and inexplicably changed positions, showing its face. It was a ghastly, pasty white. The figure then spoke two words. "October 7," it said, followed by a wrenching groan and the apparition's disappearance. There was nothing there in the darkness but the dead Ponderosa pine. The man who witnessed this strange event tried to convince himself that it was only a freak of his imagination, a trick of the darkness, but he knew what he saw. He concluded that it was the ghost of one of the men executed on the tree. What the date meant, he could not discover. No recorded execution occurred on October 7, and no event has since surfaced to make the date noteworthy. We might conclude that this first recorded supernatural occurrence in the neighborhood of the Hangman's Tree set the energy of all those victims free, explaining why events continue to make life in that neighborhood a little more than just interesting.

Chapter 2

GHOSTS ON THE GULCH

If buildings had souls, Helena would be an incredible repository for them. The community is justly proud of the flamboyant Victorian-era architecture that has survived along the gulch. The Boston, St. Louis and Atlas Blocks in particular illustrate why Helena's post-railroad architecture earned it the nickname "Queen City of the Rockies." However, during 1970s urban renewal, the city demolished more than 230 historic structures, discontinued traffic along Last Chance Gulch and created the downtown Walking Mall. Pieces and parts of vanished landmarks lie scattered like bones in a graveyard along what was once Helena's main thoroughfare. Now these remnants are ghostly reminders of the times when trolleys clanged and rumbled along the busy street.

When shadows grow long and the sun begins to set, night falls quickly over Last Chance Gulch. Darkness softens the metal features of the sculpted miners at their sluice box on the South Walking Mall. Half a block to the north, nightfall blurs the rugged profile of the heroic-size bronze sculpture *Bullwhacker*, whose airborne whip forever cracks over the ghosts of plodding oxen. Survival depended on these hardy men and the beasts of burden that carried supplies to the early mining camp. You might think that the night beckons those ghosts of so very long ago, and perhaps it does sometimes call them out. But it's my theory that the energy of our earliest pioneers has dwindled, and more recent ghosts haunt the gulch today.

There is one exception. Helena has myths and legends associated with its downtown tunnel system that once delivered steam heat to businesses from a central heating plant at Sixth Avenue and Fuller Street. Common in urban areas across the West, they are reputed to have served clandestine purposes. However, Helena's tunnels are associated with neither the Chinese nor the red-light district, as many believe, but rather they may have facilitated liquor trade and perhaps political shenanigans during Prohibition. Some basements beneath Helena's oldest buildings have bricked-in archways and filled-in openings.

A team of professional paranormal investigators from Seattle had occasion to investigate one of the basements where a speakeasy operated during the 1920s. I was a guest participant, and I vividly recall that several team members were particularly drawn to one of these filled-in archways. Several psychic team members felt strongly that in the nineteenth century, a woman had been murdered and placed in that space. She was anonymous, perhaps a prostitute whose disappearance went unnoticed. One team member claimed he could see the person who committed the crime wearing an official badge, like one a fireman or a policeman would wear. According to the team members, the woman's spirit walks the underground passages, hoping that someday her body will be found.

Helena has long battled its demons, mourned its dead and rebuilt after fires, earthquakes and other tragic events that have periodically disrupted the community. Fires especially figure prominently in Helena's past. The "Guardian of the Gulch," Helena's iconic wooden watchtower built on Fire Tower Hill, which has been watching over the town for most of its 150-year history, is one reminder; the Atlas Block on the North Walking Mall is another. Built in 1889 as an advertisement for fire insurance, its symbolism was not lost on anyone who lived through those early years when fires repeatedly claimed chunks of the community. Stylized flames lick at the building's cornice while winged salamanders—mythical phoenix-like creatures that arise reborn from ashes—play at the top. Atlas himself, at the building's center, carries on his shoulders the heavy responsibility that fire insurance guarantees.

Fire figures in the colorful history of the Montana Club. Helena's wealthy elite organized the far-famed gentlemen's club in 1885 to promote art and culture in the former mining camp. Helena became the territorial capital in 1875, but into the 1880s, it was still a rough-around-the-edges frontier outpost. Members built their first handsome and elegant club in 1893 at Sixth Avenue and Fuller Street. Ten years later, they hired Harry Anderson to run the elevator after school. In those days, elevators required operators. Fourteen-year-old Harry was the son of the club's beloved "master of

Helena's Fire Tower, the "Guardian of the Gulch," has been a community icon since 1874.
Chloe Katsilas, Rio de Luz Photography.

mixes," Julian Anderson, a former slave who tended bar from 1893 until his retirement in 1953. No one knew that Harry was an arsonist. He liked to call in the alarm and watch the excitement. Sometimes, the firemen let him help. Harry had started several fires but had never been caught.

On a snowy night in April 1903, Harry took the elevator to the sixth floor. No one was around, so he dropped a match on a pile of burlap sacks. His little fire exploded into a monster, gobbling up the building floor by floor. Investigators eventually discovered Harry's crime, and he spent the rest of his youth at the industrial school for juveniles in Miles City.

The second Montana Club rose on the same site like a phoenix. Nationally renowned architect Cass Gilbert designed the present club, where members have enjoyed elegant dining since 1905. Women have long been accepted as members, and the middle floors—once handsome quarters for its bachelor members—are now office condominiums. Tales of political deals, wild parties, illegal gambling and famous guests remain part of the club's legendary history. And there are other kinds of tales, too.

A few years ago, then manager Nord Johnson and several employees had been in the building late on a Saturday night, tidying up after a reception. When they left and locked the building, all was as it should have been. But on

Monday morning, they found one of the two elevators stuck between floors. It had not been stuck on Saturday night, so it obviously had been running in the empty building. The repairman went down to the basement, where a niche in the wall housed the gearbox. He removed the screws, pried off the heavy dust plate and discovered the problem. Stuck in a gear, holding up the elevator, was a *marble*. It's one thing to find marbles in your house, but in the gears of the Montana Club's elevator? How it could have gotten there is a puzzle that raises the question: Is Harry still around playing tricks?

Every spring, elementary students join me on tours of Helena. We explore the history and the stories behind various landmarks and neighborhoods, and the kids learn about their community heritage. In May 2012, seventy-five third graders from Rossiter Elementary School were on their annual field trip with me. The teachers planned three rotations for the three classes. One group toured the Original Governor's Mansion, one group toured Last Chance Gulch with me and the third group toured the Montana Club. And then we rotated until all three groups had visited all three places.

The present Montana Club (right), built in 1905, replaced the original building after it burned in 1903. *John DeHaas, SHPO.*

I finished with my first group, which ended at the Montana Club, and I waited for my second group to emerge. The kids burst out of the club, talking excitedly among themselves. My first group disappeared into the club, and I herded the second group along the sidewalk. Now they seemed strangely quiet. I asked if the tour guide had told them any of the club's ghost stories, and they all shook their heads no. But as we moved down the gulch, a couple of boys fell in beside me.

One of them said, "You know that place in the basement where there is that counter with a big mirror behind it?"

I nodded and said, "Oh, you mean the Rathskellar?" The basement bar is still a part of the club, furnished in dark wood to resemble a German pub. The club occasionally hosts parties and events there. Apparently the tour had finished up in the Rathskellar.

"Yeah," he said and rushed on, words tumbling out. "That place is freaky. I didn't like it. I saw a man in the mirror. He was dressed kinda funny, and when I looked around, he wasn't there in the room with us." A couple of the other boys vigorously nodded in agreement, indicating that they had seen the image too. I thought to myself that these boys were just fooling around. They probably knew I like this kind of thing, and they were just trying to impress me. So I let it pass without comment.

Forty-five minutes later, I waited at the Montana Club for the third and last group to come out and tour the gulch with me. They could not have had any contact with the previous group at all and could not have known about the image the students claimed to have seen in the Rathskellar. This group emerged, chattering loudly. Before I could even ask them if they had enjoyed the tour, one of the youngsters piped up. "We saw this weird man in the mirror. He was just standing there watching us. We looked around, and he wasn't in the room with us. He was just in the mirror and then he wasn't there anymore!" A chill went up my spine. Who was it? Some long dead club member? Harry Anderson? We will never know.

Across and a little north of the Atlas Block, the LaLonde, Granite, New York and Gold Blocks are all replacements, built after a horrendous inferno began in the wee hours of July 16, 1928. An untended pot of grease in the kitchen of the Curtis Café ignited and quickly spread. In the end, four multistoried downtown buildings lay in ruins.

The Atlas Block's message to rebuild perhaps served as encouragement to the owners whose buildings burned. Within a year, businesses, professional service providers and commercial stores moved into the four replacements. Decades passed, offices changed tenants and, by the twenty-first century, a records management firm occupied the Granite Block. Employees in the second-floor offices began to talk among themselves about voices they heard at random times. That in itself was peculiar. But even more bizarre, these were the voices of children. Why would children's voices resonate in the corridor of an office building?

Sometimes employees heard children running in the hallway, giggling, laughing and whispering. One woman found a vintage barrette, a *child's* barrette, from the 1930s or 1940s on her desk. The records this firm managed were secure, and few people had access to the offices because of the confidential information—social security numbers, insurance and medical records. She had had no visitors, and no children had been in the building. She put the barrette high up on top of a filing cabinet and forgot about it. Sometime weeks later, she was on the phone when she felt something fall off her shoulder. The hair stood up on the back of her neck as she picked up the barrette where it had fallen onto her desk. How could it have gotten from the top of the filing cabinet to her shoulder? She shivered.

For some time, the women in the second-floor offices discussed the childish voices. No one knew who the former second-floor tenants were, and they didn't really think to wonder. Research provided the answer. City directories revealed that the Whalen Studio occupied rooms upstairs in the Granite Block. Ruth Carpenter Whalen and her associate, Genevieve Looby, taught piano and music appreciation. Many Helena children took lessons at the studio, studied related subjects and performed in recitals from the time the Granite Block opened in 1929 until at least 1952. All those children, all the nervous energy those recitals sucked out of them, even after all this time, still resonates on the second floor.

During the time Mrs. Whalen's studio occupied the rooms in the Granite Block, another spectacular blaze began on a freezing cold Sunday morning in January 1944. The fire started in the elevator shaft of the Montana National Bank Building, a few doors down from the Granite Block. Eight people suffered burns and serious injuries, and the charred remains of two elderly residents were recovered from the ice-encrusted building.

The marble in the elevator gearbox at the Montana Club and the National Bank fire that began in the elevator shaft underscore the notion that elevators have a singular place in Helena's downtown history. Helena has no real skyline partly because it nestles into the gulch and can't be seen from much of a distance but also because it has no buildings taller than seven stories. In the 1890s, despite its small population of about thirteen thousand, Helena prided itself on being very cosmopolitan. Its taller buildings featured passenger elevators early on, an amenity that helped promote Montana's capital as entirely up to date. The Placer Hotel and the Power Block illustrate Helena's lofty aspirations.

The Placer got its name from the placer gold washed from the gravel during the excavation of its foundation. Completed in 1913, the seven-story, 172-room hotel was the largest hostelry between Minneapolis–St. Paul and Portland. Architect George H. Carsley designed the building in consultation with Cass Gilbert, architect of the Montana Club. During legislative sessions, the Placer was the Democratic hangout. John F. Kennedy even stayed there in 1960 on the campaign trail during the state Democratic Convention.

During its long life, the Placer hosted many events and was home to numerous prominent Helenans. Many eminent residents took apartments there later in life. Now the hotel is divided into condos, and after some years of semi-neglect, the building again has enthusiastic residents and tenants. Many have fond memories of the Placer.

An acquaintance once shared her special memories of the Placer with me. During the 1960s and 1970s, it was a treat for her to come to Helena to shop for school clothes, prom gowns or outfits for special occasions. She had many warm memories of those wonderful times spent with her mom. They always stayed at the Placer, in the same corner room. She confided to me that on one such trip, she had a most interesting experience.

She and her mom settled into their usual room and went to bed. She awakened in the night, and her eye was drawn to the rocking chair by the window. There was a figure in the chair, dressed in a red plaid shirt, rocking silently back and forth, back and forth. She thought to herself, "I must be dreaming." But no, she was certain she was fully awake.

The next morning, as she and her mom were having breakfast, she could not shake the vision of that man in the rocking chair. So she said to her mom, "I had the strangest dream last night. I awakened to see this man in our room, sitting in the rocking chair by the window. He was…" Her mom suddenly jumped in and finished the sentence, "—dressed in a plaid shirt. *I saw him, too.*"

The most commanding presence by far along Last Chance Gulch is the six-story Power Block. Like the Atlas Block, it was built in 1889, the year that Montana became the forty-first state. At the culmination of Montana Territory's long struggle for statehood, its legislature elected T.C. Power as one of Montana's first two U.S. senators. Power was a fabulously wealthy businessman who amassed a fortune freighting goods out of Fort Benton long before railroads crossed Montana Territory. Power built his business block

The Power Block, a downtown centerpiece, helped promote Helena as a cosmopolitan city. *Sketch from* Helena Illustrated, *1890.*

at Sixth Avenue and Last Chance Gulch to house his American National Bank. It is the most visible of Helena's downtown Victorian-era treasures. Willetts and Ashley of Chicago designed the building; it is a transition from the Romanesque Revival style to the newly emerging Chicago School. The rounded openings on the northeast corner correspond in number to the floor level.

The 1928 fire claimed all the Power Block's nearest neighbors; it burned right up to the building's south wall. Thanks to firefighters' efforts, the landmark survived that disaster, but some years later, the Power Block witnessed a singular tragedy. In Helena's century and a half, no event is more heartbreaking than the accidental death of teenager Helen June Tarrant in the elevator of the six-story business block.

Helen Tarrant was a bright youngster with a promising future. She was born in Roseburg, Oregon, on Black Tuesday—October 29, 1929—the day the stock market crashed, signaling the start of the Great Depression. Her parents moved to Townsend, Montana, where Helen graduated from the eighth grade in May 1943. Her classmates voted her one of the community's best citizens, and the American Legion presented her with its citizenship award. Helen was a charming girl with a kind disposition and a sweet, memorable smile. She was personable, responsible and perfect for the summer job she landed, operating the elevator at the Power Block—that is, she was perfect except for one thing: she was only thirteen. In those days, elevator cars were cages, not enclosed by solid walls as they are today. The job was not without danger.

On the evening of July 17, Helen was to finish her shift at nine o'clock, but she did not come home. Her mother searched frantically for her. The next morning, a Power Block employee discovered Helen's body wedged between the wall and the elevator on the sixth floor. A pink hair ribbon in the elevator sump helped explain how the accident happened. Police chief Arthur Parsons surmised that Helen's foot was caught between the wall and the elevator carriage as the car ascended to the fifth floor. This threw her forward and the moving elevator pinned her against the wall as it continued to the top floor.

Blame—if there was anyone to blame for the freak accident—rested on the Power Block's owner, the Helena Building and Realty Company. Child labor laws stipulated that children under sixteen could not be employed in hazardous occupations. The company pleaded guilty to a charge of violating state labor laws and paid a fine of $300. Helen June Tarrant was laid to rest in the Townsend cemetery. But she has not been entirely forgotten.

Employees in the building often discuss the elevator's odd behavior, and half a dozen individuals have shared their experiences with me. The elevator seems to have a mind of its own. If you push the button for the floor you want, the elevator often travels to a different floor, refusing to stop at the desired level. The Montana Council of Developmental Disabilities had its offices in the Power Block from 2000 to 2006. Deborah Swingley, CEO and executive director of the council, told me that she always felt there was something, some kind of energy, in the building. She recalled that she often brought Baxter, her Boston terrier, with her for company as well as security. The main office door had a bell that rang when anyone entered. The bell would sometimes ring, and the door would open, as if someone came in. The dog would growl, but there would be no one there. And then the door would close, as if someone walked out. It was spooky. And that was not all.

Deborah also recalled that the elevator did its own thing. She and her co-workers would push the button for the second floor, and the elevator would ignore the request, go up to some other floor, and stop. One day, an attorney in the building was riding with Deborah, and she mentioned how annoying it was that the elevator never took her to the floor she wanted. He told her that his aunt had been the elevator operator and had died in an accident. He suggested that Deborah try vocalizing the floor in addition to pushing the button, as long-ago passengers used to do when the elevator was operator dependent.

The next time Deborah rode the elevator up, she pushed the second floor button and said, "Two, please." The elevator took her right to the second floor. Others then began to call out their desired floors, and the elevator's random behavior ceased. Those who experienced this are convinced that Helen June Tarrant still sometimes controls the Power Block's elevator, politely waiting to be told what floor the passenger desires.

Last Chance Gulch does, in fact, have its ghosts. And it does not have to be the witching hour for residents and visitors to experience paranormal activity. Although it may not be the fabled outlaws, gunslingers, miners and others one might expect in a former mining camp, Helena's downtown is not lacking in spirited company.

Chapter 3
LILY'S LEGACY

An icy March wind scattered leftover leaves across the small lot as I eased into a parking place. I noticed the historic brick wall that encircled the yard and the hitching post and carriage step where long-ago guests alighted from horse-drawn conveyances. I also took stock of some forlorn-looking foliage—I thought they might be lilac bushes—huddled against the brick wall on the opposite side of the house. The broad front steps led me to a massive wooden door. I pushed it open and stepped inside to dark, heavily carved wood and beautiful stained glass. I felt the grandeur of this historic home. Helena attorney Bob Murdo ushered me into the handsome conference room and offered me a seat.

Bob and his law firm, Jackson, Murdo and Grant PC, have occupied the former Toole residence since 1979. And the house has quite a diverse history, enough history to make it a candidate for a good haunting. Bob asked how he could help, and I explained my mission: I was writing a book and had heard that he had some good stories he was willing to share.

I was surprised when he said, "I don't believe in ghosts." I thought then that this conversation would go nowhere, but he continued. "My wife believes though. While there is really nothing to suggest an association with the paranormal in this house, some situations we have encountered here do seem to lead in that direction."

To understand the unusual multilayered energy of the Toole Mansion, you have to understand those who resided there, those who impacted its history and the impressions they must have left behind. Joseph Kemp

Lily Toole, wife of Montana's first governor Joseph K. Toole, was a devoted mother and an avid gardener. *MHS Photograph Archives.*

Toole was Montana's first governor upon statehood, and his wife, Lily, was the first of the state's first ladies. Toole came to Montana from Missouri at eighteen in 1869. He studied law and went into partnership in Helena with his brother Edwin. From 1884 to 1888, Toole served as Montana's territorial delegate to Congress and sponsored the Omnibus Bill, which allowed Montana to apply for statehood in 1889. He served in the 1889 Constitutional Convention and subsequently was elected Montana's first governor. On May 5, 1890, Joseph married Lily Rosecrans.

Lily was a gentle soul. Born to the prominent family of Brigadier General William Stark Rosecrans of Civil War fame, Lily grew up in Ohio in a devoutly Catholic family. Her home in Cincinnati, Roccabella, was a former convent, and the general's brother was a Catholic bishop. Three of Lily's siblings entered the religious life. Lily's small, private wedding took place at the parsonage of St. Matthew the Apostle Catholic Church in Washington, D.C., not what one would expect from the general's daughter. The *New York Times* explained that Governor Toole was not Roman Catholic, and there was not time to obtain the dispensation required for a wedding in the Catholic Church.

The newlyweds were at home in Helena at 102 South Rodney Street, where Lily settled into her role as Montana's first lady. Their first son, named Rosecrans after Lily's famous father, was born in 1891. When Joseph's term was up, he returned to his law practice in Helena. The couple had two more children, Edwin Warren in 1893 and Joseph Porter in 1896. In the yard of the Rodney Street house, Lily planted an apple tree for each boy, and she planted lilacs to remind her of springtime in Ohio. A product of the Victorian era and an avid and knowledgeable gardener, Lily may have made these horticultural choices for several reasons.

Apple trees symbolize immortality, and surely Lily wished her sons long and productive lives. She chose hardy purple lilacs, *Syringa vulgaris*, perhaps because she knew they would do well in Montana. But also, it is well known that the Victorian era was a time of contradictions. In the Victorian language of flowers, lilacs symbolized both love and mourning. Some even considered it bad luck to bring lilacs into one's home. The scent of each tiny blossom, gathered into clusters, gives forth such an extraordinarily strong perfume that lilacs were sought after during wakes, to cover the scent of decomposition. More than that, Victorian custom dictated that at the end of deep mourning after the death of a close loved one, black clothing could be cast aside and lilac was an acceptable color for the transition back to normal life. But it may be that Lily simply regarded lilacs, an especially hardy plant, as a token of spring and renewal.

Lily was a devoted mother. She saw that Joseph converted to Catholicism and the children were raised Catholic. In 1898, when Rosecrans was about seven, tragedy tested the family's faith. Lily had taken him to California to visit her sister, Anita, in the hope that the climate would be beneficial to Rosecrans's delicate health. But the boy died suddenly of diphtheria. Lily later wrote that Anita held the little boy in his last moments and heroically "sang to him softly until he waked to hear the angel choirs." Three weeks later, Lily's father passed away from the shock of losing his favorite grandchild and namesake. Following the two deaths, Anita, a former Ursuline nun, studied shorthand and then came to live with the Tooles in Helena.

Anna Dolores "Anita" Rosecrans became Joseph Toole's secretary when he was elected to a second term as governor in 1900. Anita was much beloved by the Helena community. A gifted musician, on Sundays she played the celebrated Barckhoff tracker organ at the First Baptist Church after attending her own Catholic services. In 1903, Anita's sudden death from pneumonia devastated Lily and the community. Hundreds attended a memorial at the First Baptist Church. In Anita's eulogy, Reverend James McNamee called her passing "a public loss." Lily never lost her composure.

But the Tooles, especially Lily, keenly felt these losses, and they built the house on Ewing Street hoping to leave their sad memories behind. The State of Montana owned no executive residence until 1913, and so Governor Toole had to supply his own home for state functions. The Ewing Street residence was worthy. Lily, however, dreaded moving in because the house was in a vulnerable location, two blocks north of the Lewis and Clark County courthouse and the county jail.

Lily's fears were justified. The family had been in residence six months when an inmate, being escorted from the courthouse to the jail, escaped. Isaac "Ike" Gravelle was a three-time criminal, most recently convicted of extortion against the Northern Pacific Railroad. Although he received ten years' hard labor at the Deer Lodge State Prison and a $5,000 fine, many viewed the sentence as too lenient because Gravelle's escapades endangered hundreds of lives. His dynamiting spree included damaging a bridge over the Yellowstone River just before two trains, one carrying 225 passengers, traveled over the weakened tracks. Fortunately, no one was injured. Gravelle was being tried for stealing the dynamite. A fourth felony conviction could earn him a life sentence.

On August 11, 1904, as the trial was underway, the court adjourned for lunch. Someone slipped Gravelle a weapon, which he concealed as the deputy led him back to his cell at the jail. After lunch, as Deputy Anthony Korizek unlocked the cell to escort him back to the courtroom, Gravelle pulled the gun on Korizek and the jailer, a scuffle ensued and Gravelle fired three shots, mortally wounding the deputy. Taking Korizek's gun, Gravelle walked out of the jail with two weapons under his coat.

A witness in the case recognized Gravelle, and the escaped man bolted, firing over his shoulder as he ran up Breckenridge Street with several courthouse employees and butcher John Raab in hot pursuit. Gravelle ran around the corner into the Tooles' yard and took refuge in Lily's flower garden. Lily and her two boys were in a sitting room on the second story and heard the commotion. Gravelle took cover in the Tooles' basement stairwell. He tried to get into the basement, but the coal-room door was fortunately locked. Cornered, the story was that he put Korizek's gun to his temple and pulled the trigger. However, the coroner's report hints that Gravelle's death was not a suicide. No one disputes that when the firing ended, Gravelle's black heart beat no more. He lay sprawled with his head at the bottom of the steps in a pool of blood at the Tooles' basement door.

After reelection, Joseph Toole resigned as governor in 1908 due to ill health. Lily and Joseph grew older, dividing their time between Montana and California. In 1922, they sold the house and moved to the Placer Hotel. Joseph died there in 1929; Lily died a decade later in Los Angeles. Both are buried in Resurrection Cemetery in Helena.

Joseph Toole helped lay the cornerstones of the new state, but Lily made her own mark. During the construction of the capitol, as her husband oversaw the interior art, Lily aided in the landscaping and saw that many lilacs were planted over the grounds. Perhaps they were symbolic as Lily was in deep mourning for her sister. But perhaps Lily regarded lilacs as a harbinger of spring and knew that they would be hearty and live long. Whatever her reasons, the many lilacs Lily brought to Helena provided cuttings for many others, and their sweet perfume floating on the breeze in spring is her special gift to her adopted community.

The Schaeffer family next owned the Tooles' elegant home. Lincoln H. Schaeffer was a local grocer, president of the Wholesale Grocers' Association and, with his son, Dorman, operated the Schaeffer Oil gas stations. He passed away from cancer in his bedroom at the house on August 25, 1927, with his family gathered around him. After her husband's death, Margaret Schaeffer lived mostly alone in the vast house, rattling around in its many rooms, for the next twenty-five years. What was it like to wander through the elegant, empty rooms for all those years alone? One wonders if she encountered anything out of the ordinary or if she was sensitive to the imprints others before her left on the house. Perhaps she thought of Lily when the lilacs bloomed in her yard in the spring.

After standing vacant from 1957 to 1963, the house was purchased by the Catholic Diocese of Helena for use as a dormitory and headquarters for its Catholic Charities. During the 1960s, Catholic Charities in Helena took in more than sixty young Cuban refugees. These frightened, homesick children were among fourteen thousand youngsters sent to the United States by parents who feared Fidel Castro's communist regime. President John F. Kennedy determined that the children were not safe in Miami, and so they were portioned out to other places across the United States. Some of the children who came to Helena were taken in by local families, some were taken in by St. Joseph's Home and others found housing in the Toole House, at this time known as Brondel Hall.

The boys arrived at the airport speaking no English, unused to cold weather and very unsettled. What they thought would be a short stay turned into years for many of them. Boys took over rooms throughout the Toole house and basement, which was divided into a series of cubicles. These youngsters shed their childhood in the house. It isn't hard to imagine the anguish and loneliness they endured.

After housing the refugees, Catholic Charities ran Brondel Hall as a home for unwed mothers during the 1970s. These young women and the stigma society inflicted on them certainly added yet another dimension to the character of the house. In the late 1970s, the house was sold and briefly divided into apartments. Attorneys Dave Jackson and Bob Murdo then bought the property and renovated the house in 1979. Their law firm moved its offices into the house where they still maintain their practice.

Bob admits that the house does have its noises. The wind whistles through the gracious front porch and around the third-floor dormer. Hot-water

The Tooles' lavish executive residence was worthy of Montana's first family. *Chloe Katsilas, Rio de Luz Photography.*

heating pipes loudly creak and clank. Bob always liked to tell his kids and their friends that the ghost of Ike Gravelle was knocking on the pipes and roaming the basement. Bob's grown son, Damon, remembers well that as kids they loved the stories but were scared to death.

Unusual incidents added fuel to the tales. Soon after the attorneys moved in, a brick wall was being removed to add parking spaces. The backhoe uncovered a shoe and some clothing underneath a layer of concrete. The work stopped. The sheriff was called to investigate a possible crime scene. Under the sheriff's supervision, the backhoe unearthed some bones. Analysis proved that they were not human, and officials speculated that before the Tooles' built the house, the lot contained a privy or a dump. It was *almost* a good story, and although the possibilities fired imaginations, there may be a better explanation.

Historic Sanborn-Perris Fire Insurance Maps for Helena in 1884, 1888 and 1892 clearly show that there was never an outhouse or trash dump on the property. Since the items were discovered decades ago, there is no way to assess the time period of the clothing or the shoe. However, from the seventeenth through the twentieth centuries, it was a common practice to place one shoe and associated items of clothing, or even animal bones, beneath thresholds and foundations for good luck to the householder. Bad spirits or energy would fill the shoe instead of plaguing the occupants. Perhaps the family's past tragedies and Mrs. Toole's trepidations about the new house led the family to follow this tradition, hoping that their new house would bring them luck.

Another event is not so easily explained. The attorneys had a massive conference table made to fit the formal dining room. Local craftsmen made the table of two- by ten-foot oak slabs put together with C-clamps. The spectacular table—a beautiful work of art—nearly fills the former dining room. During the firm's first winter in the new quarters, Bob was alone in the house working late one night. It was about 11:00 or 11:30 p.m. and as cold as it gets in the dead of winter. Suddenly a tremendous *BANG* disturbed the quiet. Bob says that he was more than just startled. He was certain that someone had fired a shot inside the house. It brought to mind that long-ago gun battle and Ike lying in a pool of blood at the foot of the basement stairs.

Bob searched the house, inside and out, and checked the basement stairs. Nothing was amiss. Finally, he gave up. A day or two later, staff discovered the probable source of the bang. One of the boards in the new conference table had spilt, apparently with quite an explosion. That is the only explanation Bob has ever been able to come up with. But what kind of force made it do that?

While Bob has not personally experienced anything odd since the table exploded, others tell different stories. Some staff report muffled voices in the conference room when no one is in there, lights and equipment turning off or on and odd computer problems. But the basement seems to be the hot spot. Several employees have had eerie experiences there, where the firm has a library and keeps its files. One young woman was reading a file and left it sitting on the floor to run upstairs for a moment. There was no one else around, but when she returned a few minutes later, the file had disappeared. She finally found it back on the shelf, refiled.

The basement energy does seem to target younger employees, perhaps because of its connection to the teenage refugees or perhaps because teens are more vulnerable. One youngster working for the firm as a runner emerged from the basement shaking uncontrollably. He had gone there to retrieve a file and found every single door in the basement standing wide open. At first he thought someone was playing a trick, but it became quite obvious that it would have been an elaborate, time-consuming joke. Not only were all the doors to the numerous rooms weirdly and uncharacteristically open, so were the glass doors to the library bookcases, the doors to the crawl space and even the doors to the electrical box and fuse box. No one claimed responsibility.

Most recently, Helen High School senior McKaulie Matteson was working part time for the firm in the fall of 2012. She didn't much like going down to the basement, but she had to do her job. On one occasion, she had to do some filing in the very back cubicle. She headed down the stairs, flipping the first light switch up to turn on the light, and then as she made her way through the other rooms and the hallway, she flipped each switch up to turn it on. Finally she reached the back cubicle and flipped that switch up. She settled into work mode, absorbed in her task.

Suddenly the light flipped off. McKaulie felt for the switch, and it was down, in the off position. That was very odd. She stepped out into the hall just in time to see each light she had turned on blip off, one after the other. In rapid succession, it began with the light closest to her. All the way to the basement stairs, the lights blipped off, leaving her in total darkness. Panicked, she felt her way back to the stairway and bolted up to the first floor. She and another employee went to investigate. They found the breaker box on "urgent" and every switch down, in the off position. The incident defies logic.

Homes do often take on the personalities and emotions of their occupants. The Tooles' residence and its long history is a good example. And it has come full circle, from the governor—an attorney—to its present, longtime law firm. Lily and her gentle protection may perfectly balance the other unsettled energy the house most certainly has enclosed. It is not unreasonable to believe that some unpleasant spirits linger but that Lily's more benevolent energy helps safeguard the place she once called home. And remnants of the lilacs she planted in her yard still add their sweet perfume to the gentle winds of spring.

Chapter 4

THE HAUNTING OF REEDER'S ALLEY

We stood at the top of Reeder's Alley as I told my story. The wind picked up, as it almost always does when I get to the part about the birds. As if on cue, chickadees and sparrows and a couple crows began to gather in the neighboring trees. The branches clacked together as the wind riffled the leaves. Soon enough, I had to pause in my story as the birds became more insistent. It is a curiosity that, regardless of the season, birds almost always make an appearance when talk turns to Laura Duchesnay.

The quaint neighborhood goes back to the dwindling gold rush, when miners left their log cabins for better living conditions. Louis Reeder built the tiny multilevel flats, almost always home to single men, between 1873 and 1884. From the 1910s to 1933, Laura Duchesnay was one of the alley's few female residents. Her husband, George, a lineman for the Montana Power Company, owned the stone house at the top of the alley. The Duchesnays occupied the front apartment, rented out the three others and operated a string of tourist cabins.

Laura had the magic touch. She healed the injured birds local children brought to her, and she raised canaries by the hundreds in her tiny apartment. Laura died in February 1933 after a short illness. According to her February 25 obituary in the *Helena Independent*, George brought her home to Reeder's Alley. Neighbors filed into the small apartment, crowded with Laura's canaries, to pay their last respects. After that, George collected rents until he died in 1940. The memory of Laura and her songbirds faded.

Reeder's Alley originally offered miners better housing than crude log cabins. *Chloe Katsilas, Rio de Luz Photography.*

By the 1950s, male pensioners lived in the tiny apartments without running water or toilets, but they were not anxious to leave; housing for the elderly was hard to find. A few years passed, and the city had tagged Reeder's Alley for eventual demolition. Three dynamic Helena women—Eileen Harper, Jane Tobin and Pat Boedecker—purchased the stone house at the top of the alley where Laura had raised her canaries. The three women began renovations in February 1961. They removed partitions dividing the original apartments and cleared decades of accumulated refuse. They dreamed of creating a haven for artists and visitors.

When all twenty-three elderly tenants found alternative housing, the women acquired the other alley buildings. For more than a decade, artists' galleries and shops brought visitors to Reeder's Alley. The women sold their enterprise in 1973, and the stone house eventually became the Stonehouse Restaurant, one of Helena's most popular eateries. In 2002, I interviewed waitress Michaela Crawford, who shared her experiences with me. She recalled how she and most of the staff had some odd encounters, but one experience stood out.

On the night before Valentine's Day, Michaela stayed late, setting the tables for the next day. She finished her work and was almost out the front door when she heard chirping. She thought a bird was trapped in the building and knew if it flew around all night the tablecloths would be full of bird droppings. So she searched and searched. No bird. Tired and frustrated, Michaela stood at the door, her eyes shut hoping to better locate the chirping. Suddenly she heard, not one bird, but a whole flock of tiny chirping birds. She heard their wings beating the ceiling as they flew to the back dining room. The sound stopped. She never found any birds in the building.

I asked Michaela if she knew about Laura's canaries. She was quiet for a moment. Then she simply said, "No." I could tell she was suddenly aware that her encounter was extraordinary. Since then, the story has accumulated other details that complement the layered history of Reeder's Alley.

In 2000, owners Darrell and Kathy Gustin donated the stone house to the State of Montana. The building was vacant more often than not for the next eight years. During its final months as a restaurant, I went to lunch at the Stonehouse, and Michaela was again waitressing. I asked her if the birds had "spoken" to her anymore. She replied that she had not heard them recently, but she went on to say that a few weeks previous, a young boy was at the restaurant with his family. Michaela saw him come out of the restroom up front. She thought he looked upset, so she stopped and asked him if he was all right. He answered, "How come I can hear all these birds chirping? It's driving me crazy," he told her, "because no one else can hear them."

During conversion of the stone house to office space in 2008, workers removed a section of flooring to install computer wiring. Beneath the floor they found two dugout underground rooms lined with stones. The *Independent Record* reported the story on May 23, 2008. I speculated that the rooms were related to Prohibition, probably clandestine storage for moonshine. A student in my Montana history class at the University of Montana–Helena later verified it. Her grandfather had once told her that in the 1920s, you could buy bootleg whiskey at Reeder's Alley.

"People lined up at the stone house during certain times of the month," said the student, "but they feared that the revenue officer would come around asking questions. The lady who lived in the stone house would bring out cages of birds. If anyone asked why they were in line, customers would just say they were there to buy canaries."

When things happen in a place, they leave an impression. Not everyone experiences residual energy, but for those chosen few, the experience is memorable. Laura's canaries still sing their songs to those who know how to listen. And the alley has many other stories, too.

The stone house at Reeder's Alley was home to Laura Duchesnay and her canaries. *Chloe Katsilas, Rio de Luz Photography.*

Some years ago, a woman rented a space on the alley's lower level, intending to open a small craft shop. The tiny apartment contained nothing more than a room and a small closet. She had only been a tenant for a week when late on a Friday afternoon, she went to the closet to retrieve a broom. *Something* came from behind and shoved her in. The door slammed shut and locked. She spent that night and most of the next day in the closet. With a bobby pin she found in her pocket, she finally jimmied the door open. She did not return. The apartment stood empty for a long time.

Lance Foster occasionally conducted ghost walks in the neighborhood during this time. One night he decided to walk his route alone. He headed up the alley and, for no particular reason, paused in front of this apartment. He stood enjoying the quiet of the evening. Then he heard loud footsteps inside the tiny room, like someone in heavy boots, pacing back and forth. When Lance described this incident to me, I asked him if he looked in the window to see who it might be. He quickly answered, "Are you kidding? I got out of there as fast as I could!"

The agitated spirit could be Stark Evans, a huge Native American pensioner who took on the role of protector and spokesperson for the alley.

Pat Boedecker wrote that he was so protective of the alley and the women that he even shot at their husbands one night, thinking they were intruders. Evans lived in several of the Reeder's Alley apartments at different times, including the one where Lance heard the footsteps.

Current tenants have their own stories. Ted Mazzarese occupies the alley's only area that has been modernized for residential space. His three-room apartment is on the upper level and includes what were originally two larger rooms. Ted enjoys living there because he appreciates its history and often wonders about the others who lived there over time. The apartment has a good, but rather odd, ambience. He believes the space was once a dormitory housing many men at once. He firmly believes this because, as he told me, he is frequently privy to their quiet conversations. At night when he turns the lights off, he can hear different groups of men, talking in low, hushed tones. It is never loud enough to hear what they are saying. Rather, the conversations are respectfully quiet, just a kind of murmuring. The 1892 Sanborn-Perris Fire Insurance Map of Reeder's Alley supports Ted's theory. A note on the upper alley reads, "These buildings used as tenements and bunkhouse."

Then there was the garbage day incident. Ted had rushed to take his cans to the curb and realized that he missed the pickup. Tenant Jim Sobonya came up, and the two stood talking. The cans were full. They stood there for twenty minutes chatting, and Ted, perturbed when he noticed the cans were not aligned correctly for the garbage truck, went to adjust them. Jim offered to help, but when they went to move them, they were astonished to discover they were empty! How could the cans be empty when both Ted and Jim had been standing there for the past twenty minutes, and no garbage man had appeared?

The Yee Wau Cabin, the Pioneer Cabin and the Caretaker's House sit at the foot of Reeder's Alley. While the latter two were home to the first families who came with the 1860s gold rush, the Yee Wau Cabin dates to the 1870s and is Helena's only surviving dwelling associated with what was once a bustling Chinese neighborhood. Naturopathic physician Vicky Homer has long been the resident owner.

Vicky tells of a scary series of events that took place around 1985 when her children were small. Nothing out of the ordinary had ever happened in her quaint little cabin until then. But when an acquaintance committed suicide, that all changed. The man was a rancher, and Vicky had previously been a tenant of his. According to hearsay, he had terminal cancer and carefully paved the way for his suicide, creating a pattern of erratic behavior

The Yee Wau Cabin is the only survivor of Helena's once-bustling Chinese settlement. *Chloe Katsilas, Rio de Luz Photography*.

and pretended depression so that his life insurance would pay out. When he had established his supposed instability, he shot himself.

That night, Vicky felt something come into the cabin through a window. She strongly felt this presence enter her house, and she began to hear the floorboards creak, as if there was an uninvited guest. The house did sometimes creak, and the family did have cats; neither was the cause of the footsteps. The footsteps grew louder each night, until Vicky was terrified that her children would hear these intrusive noises and confirm that something was in the house that did not belong there. Her daughter was too young to be aware of the footsteps, but her son was older and later confided to his mother that the footsteps had indeed disturbed his sleep. Vicky worried herself sick over this nightly intruder. After some difficult sleepless nights, the final straw broke when Vicky was in bed lying on her side and felt the "presence" lie down next to her. It pressed itself against her back. Her blood ran cold.

She mentioned her fear to a friend who suggested that she thank the spirit for coming, assure him that she did not need his help and burn some sage and sweetgrass to clear the energy. So Vicky took that advice, and thankfully, the spirit left and never bothered her again. But the memory still makes her shiver.

Across the alley to the north, the Pioneer Cabin and the Caretaker's House sit side by side. Last Chance Creek once gurgled along, providing water for the first miners who staked their claims. The Pioneer Cabin, built in two stages, is the oldest dwelling in Helena with a documented history. Miner Wilson Butts built the back portion in the fall of 1864. Wilson's brother, Jonas, arrived in spring 1865 with his wife and three children, and they built the front portion of the cabin.

The Davenports also arrived in Helena in spring 1865. They settled in a one-room cabin next door to the south of the Buttses. The family traveled by steamboat to Fort Benton and by ox team to Helena. Sallie Davenport and her siblings came with their mother to join their father at his mining claim. One younger sibling died before the family boarded the steamboat *St. Johns* at Liberty Landing, Missouri. During the journey, Sallie and both her siblings fell victim to measles. Sally recovered, but her younger brother died at Fort Benton. Once settled in Helena, Sallie's older sister Anna lingered and died in the cabin in September.

In time, families left the cabins for better housing, and by the 1880s, the Davenports' former dwelling had been enlarged with several additions and marked the south end of the low-rent red-light district. From 1903 to his death in 1938, George Mitchell was the last resident of the Buttses' former home. History-conscious citizens purchased both cabins and created a museum in the Pioneer Cabin, where the Butts family once lived. They remodeled the Davenports' former cabin-turned-brothel and hired a caretaker and tour guide to live there. Since 1939, it has been known as the Caretaker's House. Now under state ownership, the museum in the Pioneer Cabin remains intact while the Caretaker's House is a restaurant.

Michelle and Jim Sobonya operate the Old Miners Dining Club at the Caretaker's House. They believe the cabin to be "spiritually charged." Numerous incidents have convinced them that there are unexplained forces there. Steeped in a history so diverse, it is nearly impossible to sort out whose energy might remain there. For starters, at least three people are known to have died in the tiny house. Ten-year-old Anna Davenport was the first. In 1947, Charles Warren passed away there, and in 1989, Don Sinamon suffered a fatal heart attack. Both were longtime caretakers of the Pioneer Cabin. Perhaps the events the Sobonyas have experienced are tied to these deaths, to others thus far unknown or to residual energy.

Both Jim and Michelle have had kitchen implements go missing and then turn up in plain sight. For example, a favorite glass mixing bowl Michelle uses only for making brownies disappeared from its usual place in the

The Caretaker's House (left) and the Pioneer Cabin (right) housed the first miners' families at Last Chance Gulch. *Ellen Baumler*.

cupboard. When Jim went to the cupboard to get it, the bowl wasn't there. It had not been used since the last time Michelle made brownies, and it should have been there. Finally he got out a plastic bowl. He stood wondering what in the heck happened to that glass bowl. He glanced at the sink, and there it was, on top of the dish drainer. Neither Jim nor Michelle had used it. Its resting place in plain sight defied explanation.

One day, Jim was at the stove making soup for lunch. Behind him at the sink, a spoon fell to the floor. That was odd. Jim looked at the dish drainer, thinking that maybe it was too full, but there were only four spoons sitting in the utensil cup. It could not have fallen or rolled out. He picked up the spoon, put it in the bin to be washed and turned back to the soup. Another spoon hit the floor and then another. Mildly annoyed, but amused, Jim loudly told whatever, or whomever, it was that he had lunch to get ready and could not be washing spoons all morning. He asked them to stop. The activity, at least *that* activity, ceased.

The Sebonyas have found items decorating the cabin rearranged or moved. Sometimes when they come into the restaurant, they find mirrors—not the pictures on the wall, just the mirrors—hanging slightly crooked, all leaning in the same direction. And after Michelle puts fresh flowers on the various tables, she sometimes finds a single deep pink carnation plucked from the vase, positioned on the outside in a diagonal from the other flowers. It is always the deep pink carnations that are out of place. After the third occurrence, it became apparent that this was not random.

On another occasion, Jim and Michelle were sitting quietly in the dining room, planning the weekend meals. A loud crackling and snapping sound sent them racing to the kitchen. The hot water was on full blast and splattering in the deep utility sink. Then there was the time when a visiting friend stepped out of the bathroom and attempted to shut the door behind her. She encountered resistance and hesitated. The door suddenly slammed open as if someone on the other side violently pushed it. On another occasion, Michelle was chatting with three ladies from Georgia who were dining at the restaurant. She was immersed in the conversation when out of the corner of her eye she noticed a ball of light, or orb, about twelve inches in diameter, bouncing up and down in an empty chair.

Not all occurrences are entirely benign. Michelle was in the kitchen when she had a frightening encounter that she believes brought bad energy into the house. She was alone in the restaurant baking desserts when she heard loud clomping footsteps, like someone in heavy boots, in the dining room. The footsteps came closer and closer, and finally she heard them come up the several steps into the kitchen. Michelle saw a tall cowboy standing by the sink right next to her, and his looming presence filled the small space. Although his stance was not threatening, Michelle was afraid for the first time in the Caretaker's Cabin. She felt that the cowboy was looking for someone. He wore a bright yellow shirt and cowboy hat. He was obviously from another time; perhaps he was a customer from the red-light era. As Michelle was about to scream, he turned and quickly wisped upward, right through the wall.

Michelle has had one other ghostly encounter in the kitchen. A young man, maybe in his late teens, stepped right up into her space at the kitchen sink. He wore a loose-fitting, wrinkled, brown button-up shirt. Suspenders held up what appeared to be brown wool pants. Startled and concerned, Michelle reacted by moving away from the figure. Upon her sudden movement, the young man quickly disappeared.

The Caretaker's House and the spacious backyard garden it shares with the Pioneer Cabin have a special quality. Sounds of children playing sometimes filter from the yard into the alley. Some claim to have glimpsed children waving as if to greet visitors. And sometimes, when no one is around, parlor music tinkles on the wind, drifting across the garden. The area is a gathering place where strangers have discovered coincidental connections and had various kinds of experiences. And for myself, beyond the birds appearing as if on cue, I have had my own encounters.

Some years ago, before the state acquired title to the Pioneer Cabin, only I and one other person had access to the building. Back then, both front and back doors had heavy combination locks. One morning I arrived early to give a tour to some elementary students. When I removed the padlock at the back entry, the door would not open. Puzzled, I went in through the front door to see what was wrong at the back. I couldn't believe what I saw. The back door was bolted from the inside. We never used the bolt, and no one had been in the cabin since I had been there the previous week. But someone, or *something*, had shot the bolt from the inside. In the fifteen years that I have been giving tours in the cabin, the back door has been bolted from the inside twice.

The stone house, the tiny apartments, the Caretaker's House and the Pioneer Cabin each has its own unique ambience where generations of people have lived and sometimes died. Some have left impressions on the place. Each person seems to have his or her own experience, when leftover energy or emotions clash with the present. And there is still more to tell about Helena's most historic neighborhood.

Chapter 5
A SPIRITED NEIGHBORHOOD

Neighborhoods change with every generation, and that is true of Reeder's Alley. When the pensioners moved out and artists moved in, the tenor of the quaint little area changed dramatically. Not only did the alley have customers and visitors, its rejuvenation brought a first generation of children who had the freedom to roam the alley's nooks and crannies. Children scampered up the alley, explored the hillside and played in the places that were once off limits. Discovery is an important part of childhood, and this part of Helena offered great opportunities for the children of the saviors of Reeder's Alley, as well as those of its later shopkeepers and those who lived in a little row of houses along South Park Street. One of the special places that drew these young explorers is the Morelli Bridge, the oldest timber bridge still in use in Montana. It sits at the crest of the hill overlooking Reeder's Alley.

The City of Helena built the bridge, sometimes called the Howie Street Bridge, in 1893. The massive stone supports are the work of Swiss stonemason Carlo Morelli, who lived nearby above Reeder's Alley. The bridge served as a bypass around the south end of Last Chance Gulch. Much later, the bridge was at the bottom of what teenagers in fast cars called Thrill Hill. The north approach included a steep, stomach-dropping hill. Two-way traffic traveled over the bridge until a fatal accident in the 1970s prompted the city to eliminate much of the incline and close the bridge to northbound traffic. Much to the dismay of Helena teens, Thrill Hill was no more.

Runners have encountered a ghostly lady on the Morelli Bridge. *Chloe Katsilas, Rio de Luz Photography.*

Amber Foster Ireland was one of those alley newcomers who played in the area during the late 1970s. Her mom owned a café in Reeder's Alley, and she spent a lot of time there and under the bridge, hanging around with other local kids. She recalled with a shiver a series of incidents that have stayed with her all these years. It was early summer. Amber and her gang were making their usual neighborhood rounds when they saw an old man squatting under the Morelli Bridge. During the seedy years before the transformation of Reeder's Alley, transients frequently camped under the bridge and there was still an occasional vagrant. There was something odd about this man, though, whom they had never seen before. He spooked them. They turned around and ran the other way.

The next day, Amber and her friends went back up the alley to the stone house. It was a usual stop since one of the pastry chefs there would sneak them desserts. As they stood outside the kitchen door, all the kids looked to the bridge at the same time, and the man was there again. He had not been there a moment before. He looked up, saw the kids and winked at them. It was creepy. They got their treat and ran away as fast as they could.

A couple days later, Amber and one of the boys made their way to the top of the alley and walked the short distance to the bridge. They found a little campfire built where the man had been squatting, but it had not been lit. Always before, the ground had been weedy when they played up there, but on this day, there were no weeds; the ground was bare dirt. They didn't touch anything, but Amber's friend took the opportunity to urinate on some nearby bushes. A few days later, the kids were running around, and again they saw the man squatting under the bridge. He singled out the boy who had urinated in the bushes near the campfire. Pointing his finger at him, the man shook his head *no*.

Off and on all that summer, Amber and her friends would see the man, always squatting over twigs, building a campfire. But he never lit it. Then one day, they revisited the area, and this time, it was again weedy. It was all overgrown, like the barren ground had never been there at all. Amber recalled that she and her friends sat under the bridge wondering what was going on. As they sat there, they heard footsteps on the deck overhead. Amber backed up until she could see the bridge. There was no one there, but they could still hear the shuffling. They ran back to one of the shops and then saw smoke curling up from the area below the bridge. Amber always figured the man finally got his fire started. She wondered who he was. He could have been a transient, only she vividly remembered that he was "wispy looking."

In recalling that strange summer, Amber says, "Did we have active imaginations? Maybe we did. I am very pragmatic, though, and not easily spooked. But you couldn't pay me to climb under that bridge again."

While the Morelli Bridge defines the upper west edge of Reeder's Alley, the south edge is a small shaded parking lot where a homestead once nestled against the hillside. The house was razed in the 1970s, but a beautiful stone barn that sat behind it still stands. The Morelli Bridge and the homestead have interesting connections. The house sheltered the large pioneer family of Jacob and Elizabeth Adami.

The Adamis, born in Germany, came to Helena in 1872. They arrived on the East Coast and then traveled by sea around Cape Horn to San Francisco. From there, they went overland by rail to Corinne, Utah, and then traveled by stagecoach to Helena. Jacob developed ranch properties along the upper Ten Mile Creek area west of Helena and was one of the community's first stonemasons and cement contractors. Many sidewalks in Helena are stamped *Adami*. Jacob, along with his brothers Henry and John, had several local stone quarries. One of them was west of Reeder's Alley on Mount Helena. It was during Jacob's six-year term as street commissioner that the Morelli Bridge was constructed with stone from the Adamis' Mount Helena quarry.

Jacob and Elizabeth had seven children and established a long line of descendants. After Jacob's death in 1929, Elizabeth kept house at the homestead next to Reeder's Alley until her death at ninety-four in 1943. Two more generations of Adamis lived at the homestead. Jon Axline, a fifth-generation Adami, recalled visiting his grandmother Myrtle Adami Axline at the homestead when he was a boy. Myrtle saw the alley change and decay. She told Jon that she could remember the "fancy women" sitting on the front steps of the Caretaker's House at the foot of Reeder's Alley before the women moved on around 1917.

As the Montana Department of Transportation's highway historian, Jon has not only been a longtime colleague of mine, but we have also been friends for more than twenty years. A few years ago, he invited me along on a personal adventure. He had a neighbor, Laura Spindler, who is sensitive to psychic energy. She had never cultivated her abilities previously, but she had decided she would like to hone them a bit and see what she could discover about herself.

Laura and Jon planned a visit to the old Adami homestead site and Reeder's Alley. The idea was that Laura would relay her impressions to Jon and me, and we would try to validate them. Laura was a newcomer to Montana and to Helena. She knew nothing about local history. This seemed a good learning opportunity for all three of us. Jon knows the history of his family, and I know the history of Reeder's Alley. Jon thought, and I agreed, that perhaps Laura could shed new light on our knowledge or show us some new angles of research as she practiced her skills. On the appointed day, the three of us met at the Pioneer Cabin described in the previous chapter.

We agreed to begin in the Pioneer Cabin and work our way up the alley. Given my experience with the cabin's bolted door, I thought maybe Laura would pick up energy there. I showed her a few of the museum's artifacts, but she took no particular notice. Then I showed her one of my favorite pieces: a primitive chair, a wonderful example of how our forebears recycled everything. The seat is a cutting board, so used and splintered it could not serve that purpose any longer, and the back is an oxbow, the wooden collar that went around the animal's neck and attached to the yoke. The legs are simple peeled tree branches.

I pulled the chair out from the table, and Laura put her hand on the oxbow. She thought for a moment and said, "I can see a woman sitting in this chair. This is weird. She is next to a stream, and she has a pan in her lap full of something that looks like pebbles and sand. She is picking through it. What is she doing?"

It was clear to Jon and me that she was panning for gold, perhaps helping her husband pick out tiny nuggets. Laura's impression or vision or whatever you want to call it made perfect sense. Last Chance Creek ran right along the gulch and claims once covered the area.

We moved up the alley, and Laura stopped. "There's someone talking in my ear," she said. This seemed to be her method of receiving information.

Laura listened for a few minutes and then thoughtfully relayed what she heard: "The person says that he was the one responsible for preparing bodies for burial. Like a mortician, but more than that. He says he helped with the grieving process."

Then Laura seemed to repeat word for word what the voice told her: "It is a terrible thing to lose a child. Grieving is important."

Laura slipped into third person again: "He says he took them in the wagon up the hill for burial." She turned and pointed east.

A primitive chair made from a cutting board and an oxbow are among the furnishings in the Pioneer Cabin. *Chloe Katsilas, Rio de Luz Photography.*

It was true, and she could not have known, that the first burial ground was indeed up the hill on the highest point overlooking the gulch. I immediately thought of Anna Davenport's death in the Caretaker's Cabin, discussed in the previous chapter. Perhaps this person helped the Davenport family when Anna died. Anna was one of the first buried in the cemetery on the ridge where Central School is today.

The mood now set, we made our way over to the parking lot where the Adami homestead used to sit. Laura did not know that Jon had any connection to the area. Jon said nothing about his family but pointed out a few faint remnants of a foundation. I recalled that when we first moved to Helena, the barn—converted to a residence some years ago—was an antique shop. I had admired its stonework. Jacob Adami was indeed a skilled stonemason.

"Hmmm," said Laura.

We conversed for a bit. Then Laura cocked her head. "Someone is talking in my ear. I can't quite understand him. He either has a heavy accent or a speech impediment. I can't tell which. He is short and kind of bandy-legged, and he is demanding my attention. He is very agitated. He used to live here. He says he has been misunderstood and that people didn't like him. They said he mistreated animals. He didn't. It was a misunderstanding, just because of one incident."

Laura asked Jon if he knew who this person was. Jon looked puzzled and shook his head. He wondered if it could be his great-uncle Clarence Adami. Laura seemed to be annoyed because the man was so insistent that she could get nothing else. So we ended the session.

That evening, Jon called his dad. "Did we have a relative at the homestead who people didn't like?"

Jon's dad thought a moment and then said, "Well, there was your Uncle Clarence. He was your grandmother Myrtle's twin brother. People thought he mistreated animals. He did, too. Once he picked up his dog by the tail, and the dog bit him. It served him right."

Jon was intrigued. "So, Dad, what did Uncle Clarence look like?" The answer brought a revelation.

"Well," said Jon's dad, "He was short and kind of bowlegged. Oh, and he had a speech impediment. You could hardly understand him."

This newfound family information seemed to weigh heavily on Jon. He wanted to somehow put Clarence to rest and thought it would be a good idea to find Clarence's grave. So he asked Laura to accompany him out

Clarence Adami, photographed in 1926, believed he was unfairly judged. *Jon Axline.*

to Forestvale Cemetery, where the Adamis are buried. Jon had visited his grandparents' graves many times, but he had not come across Clarence's. However, they easily found the tombstone, and as before, Clarence began talking to Laura, insisting that that he had been misunderstood.

Laura's puppy had recently died, and she had brought his collar, which she placed on Clarence's grave, as if to say, "We understand you, and you need to let it go now. Take care of this puppy, to prove that people were wrong."

This seemed to satisfy Clarence. His voice was finally silent.

On the way back to the car, a curious thing happened. Cutting through the cemetery to reach the driveway, Laura suddenly stopped and cocked her head. "Hold on," she said, "I need to listen to this person."

They stood among the Carleton/Pyle/Sligh family tombstones. This family is of interest to both Jon and to me because of an event in 1922. Both of us have studied and written about this case, so while the interruption was a digression from Jon's own family concerns, its randomness is a real testament to Laura's abilities. She could not have known anything about this family's tragedy.

Laura felt someone tugging her, keeping her from moving toward the car. "I didn't do it! I didn't do it!" a woman's voice kept repeating. Looking at Laura's position, it was clear to Jon whose voice this was. Then Laura heard another voice chiming in. This second person reinforced the first with a definitive clue.

"Margaret was a good girl," said the female voice. "She did not do what they said."

This voice—later identified as Sarah Sligh—confirmed what Jon already suspected. The first voice was Margaret Carleton, whose tombstone lay next to Laura's foot. Sarah Sligh was Margaret's aunt. Margaret achieved notoriety in 1922 when both she and Reverend Leonard Christler—rector of St. Mark's Episcopal Church in Havre—died of gunshot wounds amid rumors of an affair. Christler's wife, Anna, present when the shots were fired, was hardly questioned. The blame immediately fell on Margaret, who officials determined shot the minister and then herself. Questions, however, remained. Laura's conversation strengthened Jon's and my suspicions that the murderer was not Margaret but Mrs. Christler. Laura had never heard of any of these people.

Jon has reconciled his experience with his Uncle Clarence and gained a much deeper understanding of his family ties. He feels that he has helped settle some family business and put Clarence to rest. We both have the greatest respect for Laura and her gift. As for Reeder's Alley, it has special meaning for Jon, not only because of his ties to the homestead site, but also because of the Morelli Bridge. As highway historian, he has written about it and thus brought the venerable icon deserved recognition. But the stories about the Morelli Bridge are not quite finished. There is yet one more tale to tell.

Stacy (not her real name) is an avid runner and has taken a route over the Morelli Bridge for the past twenty years. She told me that she has had three odd encounters that deepen the mystery and mystique of the historic landmark. The first time, Stacy only heard footsteps. Approaching the bridge from the south heading north, she swiftly crossed the bridge as she always did. This time, though, something was different. She passed no one on the road as she swept across the worn timber. But she heard "click, click, click" as if someone was walking across the bridge, heels sounding on the wooden deck. Stacy crossed the bridge and looked over her shoulder to make sure. There was not a soul anywhere.

Two years passed, and it was 1999 or 2000. Stacy was running with a friend. As they approached the bridge from the south, both heard heels clicking on the timber bridge before they saw anyone. As they crossed the bridge, a figure was suddenly there, her footsteps matching the sound that had announced her. She was in her twenties, her hair pulled back in a high bun, and she wore a full dress with a big petticoat. She walked with purpose, as if she knew where she was going. As the runners approached her, she made eye contact with them and looked at them as she kept walking. Both runners saw her, plain as day.

After they had passed by and were out of earshot, Stacy's friend exclaimed, "My God! How could you be dressed like that?" When they looked back, the woman wasn't there.

Another ten years went by. On this winter day, Stacy was alone, and the road was slick, so she had to slow down. Approaching the bridge from the south, she heard the "click, click click" of footsteps on the wooden bridge. The footsteps always came before she saw the figure. As Stacy ran across the bridge, out of the corner of her eye, she saw the petticoat and felt the figure go by, closer to the top of the hill than before, on the north end of the bridge.

Stacy's three encounters with the woman in the petticoat raise questions that have no answers. Who was she? Did she live near the bridge? Did her life end somewhere nearby? Have others seen her, too? Stacy once asked the occupants of the house nearest the bridge if they had seen the lady in the petticoat. They looked at her as if she were crazy.

A transient making campfires, a grief counselor from long ago, a family member in need of peace, a lady in a petticoat—they are characters from other times that converge in the Reeder's Alley neighborhood. Most of them today are anonymous, their identities impossible to trace. But they do prove that when you are in the right place at the right time, when past and present planes converge, amazing things can happen.

Chapter 6

FOR FERN

Some believe ghosts most often appear in the dark of night, at the witching hours between midnight and three o'clock in the morning. But a group of fourth-graders disproved that fallacy firsthand in an event that neither they nor I will ever forget. It was May 24, 2012, a bright and sunny afternoon late in the school year. Some sixty fourth-graders from Helena's Four Georgians Elementary School were exploring Benton Avenue Cemetery. Teachers Kelley Bundt and Terry MacLaurin, along with parent volunteers, followed the groups of students as they spread out over the grounds. We had spent the day touring Helena's historic landmarks, and the cemetery made a great final stopping place for the kids as they walked back to their school at the end of the long day.

Benton Avenue Cemetery, listed on the National Register of Historic Places, is a wonderful classroom in which the children not only learn about the pioneers buried there but also discover Helena's interesting interment history. Established in 1870, Benton Avenue was not Helena's first cemetery. The mining camp buried its first dead in 1865 on the settlement's highest ridge, overlooking the gulch. The vantage point was so significant that city fathers moved the mining camp cemetery ten years later so that the first graded school could be built on that site. A second incarnation of Central School still occupies that same spot. Workers moved the disinterred remains to Benton Avenue, which then became the city's Protestant cemetery.

Statehood in 1889 and Helena's desire to become the permanent capital necessitated a larger, formally landscaped cemetery for its prominent citizens. Forestvale Cemetery, founded in 1890, became the favored burial place. Benton Avenue, however, is historically important for its informal plan, fenced family plots and historic tombstones that include early wooden markers and various types of mail-order and locally crafted headstones.

I had enjoyed these outings with the Four Georgians fourth-graders for a number of years. The kids were great, as always. But summer vacation was fast approaching, and they were full of energy, even after a full day's field trip. I had done my tour of the historic burial ground, and the kids had finished the root beer floats parents had provided. There was nothing about the day that was out of the ordinary at all—that is, until three girls came running toward us from the cemetery's north side. Parents Lynn and John Boughton and I were standing in the center of the old wagon road that divides the property into four sections. We saw the three girls running and sensed something was wrong. Anna Boughton and her two friends were out of breath and visibly shaken. One of them, nearly in tears, blurted out, "I saw a girl over there." We adults didn't get it at first.

"What do you mean?" we questioned her. "What girl?"

"Over there! Under the tree, I saw her, and then she wasn't there anymore," said Anna's friend.

Fern Marie Wilson favors this tree near her tombstone in Benton Avenue Cemetery. *Ellen Baumler.*

We questioned her further. "Was she a little girl? Did she see you? What did she look like?"

We began to realize what she meant as the answers tumbled out: "She was a teenager. She was sitting under the tree over there, wearing a yellow dress. She didn't see us. She had a strange look and was staring straight ahead."

We asked if they had noticed who was buried there in the area. All three girls shook their heads no. "We were too scared to look!" they said.

It seemed apparent that only one of the girls had actually seen the teenager under the tree. Lynn and John, however, knew the girl and believed that she would not make up such a story. She certainly had no reason to manufacture a tale like that. Lynn went over to check out the tombstones. She came back in a few minutes with a revelation that gave us all chills.

"There's a tombstone over there near the tree," said Lynn. "The person buried there is Fern Marie Wilson. She died in 1911, and she was fifteen years old. "

That seemed incredible. The girls had not been to that area and could not have had any preconceived ideas about who was buried at the cemetery's north edge. Who was Fern Marie? And what happened to her? And why would she appear to a fourth-grader on a field trip on this sunny afternoon?

I could not wait to get to back to my office at the Montana Historical Society and the Research Center library. It did not take long to discover what happened to Fern Marie. I found her and her date of death listed in Charleen Spalding's *Benton Avenue Cemetery*. My good friend Charleen is a fantastic researcher whose book contains dates of death and short biographies of most of the folks interred at Benton Avenue. While I did find Fern's death date and a short note about her family, there was curiously no more information. If there were something to be found about her, surely Charleen would have noted it unless she had a reason to suppress the details. So I went to the local newspaper microfilm. I found a string of articles that divulged the circumstances of Fern's death. It was not a pretty story, and Charleen—always careful about revealing delicate personal or sensational information—had good reasons for not including it. Headlines speculated that Fern had committed suicide over a love affair.

I kept thinking about Fern. If she actually appeared to the fourth-grader, why did she? I could only conclude that Fern felt overlooked and that she wanted attention, wanted to be remembered, and perhaps she had reason to want to set the record straight. I asked Charleen what she knew, and she actually did not recall Fern. But her curiosity got the better of her, and soon

Charleen provided me with a copy of the coroner's inquest into Fern's death. The pieces began to fit.

Fern Marie Wilson was a vivacious, lovely teenager with raven hair and dark eyes that sparkled when she bantered with the young men at her grandmother's boardinghouse. All the boarders vied for her attention, and she gave it freely—so freely that she might have caused some to talk. Yet no one seemed to suspect how much that talk might have hurt or what demons Fern kept within her. In 1911, fifteen-year-old Fern Marie Wilson was not so very different from teens today. She had the same timeless problems involving disconnected family and relationships that sometimes confront fifteen-year-olds. And she wanted to be older and told her friends she was sixteen.

Marie Fern—her given name—was born on June 5, 1896, to sixteen-year-old Rose Johnson. Marie preferred to call herself Fern or Fern Marie. When she was seven in 1903, her mother married Nels Wilson, and Fern took his last name. The identity of Fern's biological father is undocumented. The 1910 census records the Wilsons living in Salt Lake City, where Nels was a porter in a saloon. By the time Fern was fifteen, she had lived in several places, including Missoula, where she attended the Sisters' Academy. Much of her life, however, was spent in Helena.

Fern's mother and Nels Wilson separated and divorced, and Rose moved to Lewistown in March 1911. Fern did not accompany her. Rose's health had been poor. We can only speculate that perhaps she distanced herself from her daughter for health reasons. Nels, however, was the only father Fern had ever known, and the family breakup was certainly a major disruption. When her mother moved to Lewistown, Fern went to live with her aunt, Mary Appmann, in Helena. She was unhappy there, and after some weeks, she moved in with her older cousin, Gertrude Appmann, who lived north of the railroad tracks in the Sixth Ward. But Fern and her cousin did not get along, and so sometime late in May, Fern moved into her grandmother's nearby boardinghouse.

The close-knit neighborhood known as the Sixth Ward, northeast of Last Chance Gulch, has a distinct character even today. It was a melting pot of immigrants who came to work for the Northern Pacific or establish small businesses. The area took root when the Northern Pacific Railroad steamed into Helena in the summer of 1883. Officials located the depot nearly a mile away from downtown, thinking that the main commercial center would eventually resettle near the rail yards. That idea never quite caught on, but the bustling Sixth Ward supported several hotels, saloons, groceries, meat markets and other services catering to travelers, blue-collar workers and railroad men. During the early twentieth century, nine passenger trains stopped every day at the Union Station, and neighborhood boardinghouses overflowed with Northern Pacific employees.

Mrs. Elizabeth (Johnson) Kelley, Fern's grandmother, was born in England and immigrated to the United States with her first husband, coal miner David Johnson, in 1880. David died, leaving her with a household full of children and grandchildren whom she supported by working as a cook. She married John Kelley in 1903. He worked for the Northern Pacific as a watchman at a nearby crossing, and Mrs. Kelley ran a small boardinghouse at 1537 Walnut. It was hard work, and Fern sometimes helped the girls her grandmother hired to clean, clear the tables and do the dishes.

Elizabeth Kelley's boarders were typically young, single railroad men and therein lay the problem for Fern. Posterity has not recorded the circumstances of Fern's birth, but the 1900 census indicates that Fern's mother, Rose Johnson, was single and only sixteen when Fern was born. The two lived in Helena with Elizabeth—Rose's mother—before she married her second husband, John Kelley. Fern's extended family relationships were thus complicated.

John Kelley characterized Fern as a lively girl with a kind disposition whose laughter frequently rang through her grandmother's boardinghouse. She enjoyed the company of the young men who boarded there. Soon after Fern moved in, Rose wrote a letter from Lewistown to her daughter in Helena. The tone of the letter was very affectionate, but Rose warned her daughter to look out for the railroad men, to stay away from them and be a good girl. Rose undoubtedly recalled her own experience, giving birth at Fern's age. And these railroad boarders were men in their twenties and thirties, much older than Fern.

The days went by, and Fern missed her mother. They had never been separated for this long, and it upset Fern that she had no more letters from Lewistown. She began to think that her mother had forgotten about her, and Fern worried that maybe her mother didn't love her anymore. In retrospect, her friends and family believed that Fern was homesick and despondent over her mother, but she always maintained such a cheerful demeanor that no one suspected the depth of her anguish.

Fern went to the movies with Gust Olson, one of the boarders at Mrs. Kelley's. She celebrated her "sixteenth" birthday on June 5 (she was actually only fifteen) and accepted gifts, including a bottle of perfume and a silk handkerchief, from several of the young men. She also received a postcard photo of Fred Kaskin—another boarder—after she hinted to him that she wanted his picture. Each time Mrs. Kelley saw Fern talking with one of the young men, which was quite often, she chastised her granddaughter, telling her to stay away from the boarders. John Kelley testified that his wife was always nagging her.

When questioned about Fern's demeanor on June 16, Fred Kaskin recalled that the last time he saw Fern he knew something was very wrong. She was sitting in the rocking chair on the boardinghouse porch. He said hello to her, and she did not respond in her usual cheerful manner. In fact, she stared ahead and did not speak at all. Mrs. E.H. Brown, the Kelleys' neighbor, said that she saw Fern on the afternoon of June 16 with several of Mrs. Kelley's boarders. They were sitting on the branches of a large tree in the front yard of the boardinghouse. According to Mrs. Brown, Fern was chatting happily with the young men.

"She was washing her head," said Mrs. Brown. "I asked her what she was doing, and she said she was getting ready. And I asked her where she was going, and she said up to heaven."

No one recognized these warning signs or thought it strange when Fern said she was going to the neighborhood drugstore to get some medicine. She purchased twenty-five cents' worth of carbolic acid, which the druggist sold her without a prescription and without question. Fern returned to the boardinghouse and went straight to her room.

Julia Nikovito, who worked for Mrs. Kelley, testified that Fern was there only briefly before she suddenly burst out, saying that she was sick. Fern ran outside to the yard and lay on the grass. She showed Julia the white burns on her lips from the poison. Dr. W.A. Peek was called, but by the time he arrived, Fern was unconscious. He found white burns on her right hand, lips and in her throat and trachea, and her face was blue. He flushed her stomach with alcohol and administered stimulants and compresses—accepted treatment for poisoning—but Fern died several hours later from internal burns. She left three notes, which Mrs. Brown found in Fern's pocket.

The first note was to her grandparents. Mr. Kelley testified that his wife—who was too ill to attend the inquest—read the note, tore it up and threw it into the stove. It said something to the effect that despite what some thought, Fern was a good girl and had kept her distance from the boarders. Mr. Kelley quoted Fern's exact words from memory: "I go before God and can say that I never slept with a man in my life." Mr. Kelley said that he believed his wife had been overly strict with Fern and that was the reason for her rash action.

The second note was to her friends. "Dear All, Goodby—may you talk about me all you want," Fern wrote, "but I take a dying oath I kept my honor and those who say I never, God will prove I hope for my sake, different. Your most loving friend, Fern."

The third note was to her mother. "Dear Mother," Fern tried to explain, "I know this will be a shock, but rather than have myself knocked around any longer I am going in search of the other side. Your loving Fern."

Fern's solution to her problems was horrific and extreme. I later walked the area around her grave with Shanda Tompkins, a friend and psychic, to try to put it all in perspective. I had been careful not to reveal any of Fern's story to Shanda, but she knew immediately what had happened to the teenager and related much of the history I have just described. She also added some further details about Fern, including a more complete description of the yellow dress. Shanda said it was covered in white lace and that Fern was very proud of it. She also said that Fern was mischievous, enjoyed hanging around the tree and was not likely to go anywhere.

Two years after Fern's sudden appearance to the fourth-grader, on May 16, 2014, I was again with several classes of Four Georgians fourth-graders at the Benton Avenue Cemetery. Kelley Bundt asked me to tell Fern's story. I did, but I gave the students few details as I did not want to scare them. I told them that Fern had committed suicide by taking poison. I pointed to the tree and said that she had appeared that one time sitting beneath it and that she wore a yellow dress, and that was all.

Fern Marie Wilson took her own life in 1911. *Chloe Katsilas, Rio De Luz Photography.*

The students then had time to wander around the cemetery. Some fifteen kids headed over to Fern's tree. A few minutes later, as I approached the group, I could see that they were milling around, oddly quiet. One of the boys ran up to me. "They saw her!"

"Saw who?" I asked.

"That girl. They said she was sitting in the tree."

I thought this was highly unlikely, but I addressed the group. "Raise your hand if you saw her."

Half a dozen kids raised their hands. I asked them what they had seen. They described the yellow dress, but several of the girls offered another detail.

They said that white lace covered the top and the bottom of the dress, a detail Shanda noted but they could not have known. Then they described exactly how Fern was sitting in the tree. I recalled that she had been sitting in the tree in her grandmother's yard just before she bought the poison. The kids also said that she was just staring, her head slightly cocked. One youngster followed me as I headed back to the cemetery gate.

"She was so awful pale," he said, shaking his head and shivering. "It really gave me the creeps."

I had hoped this story would put Fern's spirit to rest. But maybe that is not what she wants.

Chapter 7

DEAD MEN WALKING

The mare stood nervously as if she knew her reaction would cause a profound event in the life of the man standing on the wagon behind her. The teamster held the reins in check as she tried to sidestep. The man on the wagon muttered—more to himself than to the crowd gathered around. His venomous anger at his enemies and at those about to bring him to justice went unexpressed, like a burning ember before flames erupt. The mare could not see that the man standing on the wagon had a noose around his neck. It lay slack beneath his shirt, against his skin. The crowd parted, and the teamster cracked his whip. The startled mare gave a tremendous lurch, and with her forward jolt, the wagon no longer had a passenger. The mare, now a runaway, barreled down the gentle slope; her hoofs pounding the rocky ground beneath her in a cloud of dust. In the few moments before bystanders stopped the mare's flight, the man's life abruptly ended. His boots dangled over the ground, and he swung lifeless on the lower branch of the Hangman's Tree. The only sound over the hushed crowd was the creaking of the rope as it cut a deep groove into the tree's lifeless branch.

That was how they did it, at least ten times with some variation, in the now residential neighborhood in South Central Helena. Two decades later in the 1880s, houses sat along Davis Street, in what had been the pathway of the frightened runaway horse. Pockets of that long-ago strange and violent energy seem to have an influence even today, especially in one particular household. All families experience hard times, but this family endured horrific grief. Whether it was a reaction to the lingering horrors imprinted on the neighborhood in the wake of so much violence or something else is open to interpretation. For the Hames family, all that matters is the terrible heartbreak they suffered and the legacy their own tragedies bequeathed. Current generations are still trying to make sense of it all.

Dominick and Angelica "Mary" Hames emigrated from Luxembourg in 1888. They began the long voyage across the Atlantic with two small daughters. Much later in life, Katherine—who was then three—dimly recalled her younger sister's death aboard the ship, her burial at sea and the sadness it caused her parents. The family settled in Helena, where Dominick found ready employment at his trade as a stonemason. A building boom, brought on by the advent of the Northern Pacific Railroad in 1883, promised steady work for skilled tradesmen like Dominick. He quarried the stone and helped to build the Presbyterian Church, the Power Block, St. Charles Hall at Carroll College and other landmarks. Six of the Hameses' eight children survived to adulthood, attesting to the hardy constitutions of the family members. Two sons, Peter and Antone, remained in Helena, where Peter was a house painter and Antone a city policeman.

The house on Davis Street had already sheltered others when the Hames family moved in. Antone and his wife, Elsie, raised their four children in the house. Their oldest son, Antone W., brought his bride, Judith, to live with the family, and they raised a third generation in the house. Antone A. (Tony) was born in 1945, Judith (named for her mother) in 1947 and Helmer in 1949. The first tragedy devastated the family.

On the afternoon of November 6, 1958, Mrs. Hames's sister, seventeen-year-old Sonja Anderson, was babysitting the two younger children. Tony, then thirteen, came home in good spirits and went upstairs to his room on the second floor at the back of the house. Tony was fascinated by the great Houdini and had carefully studied the tricks of the famous escape artist. He constantly practiced these tricks and made up his own, especially tricks with ropes.

At five o'clock, Sonja went upstairs to check on Tony. She found him face down on his bed, entangled in a quarter-

Family patriarch Dominick Hames emigrated from Belgium. *Diana Stewart.*

inch rope. The rope had been tied to the head and foot of the bed and looped around the boy's neck. A sweatshirt was tied around his head as a blindfold, apparently to make the trick more difficult. Mrs. Hames arrived home at about this time, untied the rope and began artificial resuscitation. A physician arrived and continued attempts to resuscitate the boy, but it was too late. Coroner Dave Middlemas theorized that Tony panicked when the rope around his neck tightened. The official cause of death was accidental strangulation.

The grim event cast a pall over the family and the other two siblings, Judith and Helmer. They grew up in the wake of this family tragedy. As the siblings dealt with their older brother's gruesome death, they naturally discussed the details. These discussions led to a macabre pact between them. According to family members, they solemnly promised each other that if either of them ever considered suicide, strangulation would not be an option. This pact between siblings may seem strange, but it was a way the children dealt with their grief. The promise was so intensely genuine that the next tragic event was not only profoundly horrific but also double-edged. Judith had not forgotten the chilling promise between herself and her brother.

Helmer was a fun-loving teenager who always had many girlfriends. Photos and prom pictures from the 1960s stored in family albums show him as a tall, six-foot-three young man with sandy short-cropped hair, glasses and a wide smile. His sparkling personality comes through, captured and preserved through the lens of a Kodak camera. Longtime family friend Carol Aronen knew him well, and she remembered him as a fine young man.

After graduation from Helena High School, Helmer joined the U.S. Navy and served as a petty officer on the USS *Buchanan*, a guided missile destroyer. From 1963 to 1972, the *Buchanan* and its crew took part in much of the Vietnam War by providing naval gunfire support for ground troops, reconnaissance and attacks of areas north of the DMZ. North Vietnamese artillery twice hit the *Buchanan*, in 1968 and again in 1972. It was the only U.S. deep-water warship to be hit by enemy fire twice.

According to the Hames family, when Helmer was home on leave, he told his parents that he had concerns about his safety on board the ship. There was some trouble with his crewmates, and Helmer seemed to think that someone had it in for him. On August 30, 1969, the *Buchanan* was docked at the naval base at Sasebo, Japan, for regular maintenance upkeep. The ship was preparing for departure to its home base at San Diego when horrified crew members discovered Helmer's body hanging in a small, unused utility room. There were questions from the beginning, but the death was officially ruled a suicide by hanging. The body was shipped home to Helena, where Helmer had a graveside military funeral. His parents never spoke about his death. Whenever Helmer's suicide came up in family conversation, they became oddly silent.

Soon after Helmer's shocking death, Carol Aronen, who was Judith's best friend from childhood, had an eerie encounter. She was in her bedroom in her family home on Dakota Street when she saw a very tall man standing in the room, looking at her. Almost immediately he was gone. In retrospect, Carol recognized the tall figure as Helmer Hames. She felt that something wasn't right about Helmer's death. She recalls that Mrs. Hames was always fiercely, even unreasonably, protective of her daughter, Judith, her only surviving child.

Decades later, Judith and her husband, police officer Bruce Stewart, were the fourth generation of the Hames family living in the Davis Street house. The Stewarts' daughter, Diana, was about nineteen when two episodes in the house eventually led her to research Helmer's death. Both times she

Helmer Hames (third row, second from left) died aboard the USS *Buchanan* under mysterious circumstances in 1969. *Diana Stewart.*

felt a very powerful menacing presence. The second experience was very scary. Diana was on the living room floor, awake but resting quietly. She felt something, or someone, straddle her stomach. The entity hit her hard in the chest, and it cried out in a deep voice, "I am not going to take this anymore." Diana immediately thought of her two uncles and how they had both died of strangulation. She panicked and cried out for her father.

Bruce leapt out of bed, and when he saw Diana on the living room floor, he could tell something was there. He instinctively knew that it was evil. He felt a current, like a lightning bolt, run through the room and into the kitchen. It made a loud noise that was entirely out of place. It sounded like pounding hoofs running through the house, first through the living room, then through the kitchen and into the bathroom. There, the sound seemed to disappear down the toilet. Bruce does not make light of this incident, but he does chuckle. At the time, he thought of the cloven hoofs of the devil and thought it fitting that whatever it was went down the toilet. Bruce admitted, "It was some incident!"

Diana always felt a strong connection to her uncle Helmer, whom she had never known except through the pictures in the family albums. The fright Diana experienced in the Davis Street house prompted her to question her mother and probe into Helmer's death. Judith told Diana about the pact she had made with Helmer, that if either sibling contemplated suicide, hanging would not be an option. It was a promise Judith and her brother had intended to keep.

Diana was further intrigued, and after several requests for Helmer's naval records, she finally received the reports. She feels that many questions regarding the circumstances of his death have been left unanswered. According to official documents, Helmer was found in a partial kneeling position. He was inches taller than the ceiling. His buttocks were two inches off the floor and his feet were bound. The circumstances hardly point to suicide.

Diana tracked down a former shipmate of Helmer's. In a conversation with him, she learned that many considered the death suspicious. The shipmate claimed that when Helmer's body was found, he had a forehead abrasion or "pump knot"—another term for "goose egg." And that was not all. He also claimed that when the ship docked at San Diego on September 18 and the men dispersed in different directions, the crewmate's partner suddenly shouted, "Hames!" The partner was certain he saw Helmer getting on a bus. Sailors are, admittedly, a superstitious lot. But Helmer's shipmate confided in Diana that after Helmer's death, many men including himself, believed the ship was haunted.

In June 2000, the USS *Buchanan* was one of four decommissioned ships sunk as target practice at the Pacific Missile Range off the coast of Kauai, Hawaii. The other three readily went down. But the torpedo aimed at the *Buchanan* malfunctioned, and the ship stayed afloat all night. It took another two hundred pounds of explosives for the *Buchanan* to sink, carrying its secrets and perhaps the spirit of Helmer Hames to the bottom of the Pacific.

Diana Stewart says that she believes the government paid her grandparents for their silence. Mr. and Mrs. Hames never wanted Helmer's death investigated, despite the fact that there were many reasons to discount his death a suicide. Diana remembers her grandparents' odd silence on this topic. Carol Aronen says that she believes Helmer stumbled onto something and thus knew something he was not supposed to know.

The coincidence of two strangulation deaths in the same family is strange enough, but this coupled with the history of the neighborhood that sheltered five generations of the Hames family leads to speculation. Did that early violence somehow influence Tony and Helmer or the house on Davis Street?

The house passed out of the Hames family when Bruce and Judith Stewart sold it to new owners. The new owners claimed to have also experienced supernatural events. They knew nothing about the previous occurrences but told the Stewarts that they had a puppy that unexpectedly began to bark early in the mornings. They could never determine why the puppy barked or what was disturbing it. Then one morning they heard a very loud male voice tell the puppy to shut up. They said the voice was so loud it sounded as if it were in the very same room with them. There was no one else around.

These owners also showed the Stewarts some odd photographs they had taken of the second floor. One of them, of the upstairs room where Tony died tangled up in his ropes, showed a bolt of light—like a streak of lightning—running through the photograph. Subsequent owners removed the second story and replaced it completely with a brand-new floor plan. Perhaps they, too, had unsettling episodes.

Bruce Stewart and his daughter, Diana, remain impacted by their experiences in the house on Davis Street. While interviewing the two of them, we discussed in detail the pounding hoofs that shook the house on that night some years ago. Neither Bruce nor Diana knew of the executioners' methods in carrying out the hangings on the infamous tree. But when they heard how the victim, standing on a wagon, was launched into eternity, it seemed to make some sense. The spot where the tree once stood was clearly visible from their backyard, and the house would have been directly in the downhill path of the runaway horse.

This 1875 panoramic view of Helena is the only known map showing the approximate location of the Hangman's Tree (at left). *MHS Research Center.*

Family members all admit that the upstairs bedroom where Tony died entangled in his ropes never felt right. And Bruce says that he never felt comfortable in the house, that it always had a very heavy, even sinister, feel. Considering the history of the neighborhood, this is not too surprising. While some of the victims of the hangman's noose might have been innocent, some of them were very bad, very angry men. At the moment when the rope went taut, all that fury must have hit the earth like a lightning bolt. Such malevolence could never dissipate nor could those men ever rest in peace.

Chapter 8

SOMETHING EXTRA

The Christmas Gift Evans House on Helena's lower West Side has witnessed community milestones and sheltered numerous generations. Restless and benign spirits that some believe inhabit the home seem to exist side by side. They carefully pick and choose to whom they reveal themselves and in what manner. Many former residents have related their own personal encounters, and each person's experience is unique.

The house was built circa 1877, when Helena was the newly designated territorial capital. Those who made fortunes in mining, freighting, livestock and business investments eyed the new capital as a potential place to settle. Wealthy residents began to invest in real estate. Although this house is not a mansion, its gracious lines and rich details suggest owners of financial stability. Mature vegetation nearly hides it from view in the spring and summer, but the fine roofline with its ornamental wrought-iron tracery commands a second look from passersby.

Some call this area the "Mansion District." Many who live in the neighborhood insist that not everyone lives in mansions and that "West Side" is a preferable term. While sprawling residences once stood alone on entire city blocks, smaller homes have filled in some of these open spaces. Brick sidewalks border trec-lined streets, and spectacular architecture never fails to delight visitors. Nineteenth-century owners spared no expense on expert craftsmanship and elegant furnishings that made the West Side unique to Montana in extravagance and luxury. Occasional decorative hitching posts, carriage houses and other outbuildings recall another, more gracious time.

Many have encountered the supernatural in the Christmas Gift Evans Residence. *Chloe Katsilas, Rio de Luz Photography.*

Business partners John B. Sanford and Christmas Gift Evans were among the first to build their homes on the West Side's lower edge. The partners established Helena's first water-powered sawmill in 1865 and built up a successful business selling hay, grain, flour, lumber, coal and heavy agricultural equipment. Both partners located their homes near their extensive lumberyards, which spread over several blocks at the north end of Last Chance Gulch. Sanford built his home in 1877, and a few years later, he and Evans switched houses. The home that Sanford built became the longtime residence of the Evans family.

Christmas Gift Evans was born at Deerfield, New York, in 1840 on Christmas Day. His parents felt so blessed at his birth that they considered him a gift and named him accordingly. Evans, known to his friends and associates as "Chris," was a twenty-one-year-old seeking adventure when he took the treacherous journey via Panama to San Francisco in 1862. There he found the California diggings moderately lucrative and, after a year, returned to New York. The West beckoned, however, and in 1864, he set out for Montana with a team of oxen. En route, his small party met John B. Sanford, and they traveled together. The two became lifetime friends and partners.

Chris Evans married his first wife, Margaret Graham, in 1880, and in 1883, the couple made the switch with Sanford and settled into the stunning French Second Empire–style home. After fourteen years of marriage in 1894, a kidney disorder claimed the life of Margaret Evans. The couple had no children.

In 1896, after a suitable period of mourning his first wife, Chris Evans married again. Bertha Bellis was from Liverpool, England, the daughter of a sea captain. The second Mrs. Evans brought a special grace to the house and presided over it with care. Children also blessed their home. The couple's daughter was born in 1897. In a strange twist, they named her Margaret, an odd reminder of Evans's first wife. A son, Lewis, was born in 1901. The children grew up in the house with indulgent parents who doted on them.

In January 1915, Evans caught a bad cold that led to pneumonia. By spring, he was still not himself and had developed cellular edema—a severe buildup of fluid—in his leg. This circulatory problem worried Dr. E.S. Kellogg, who determined that amputation was the only course.

Community opinions were divided over Dr. Kellogg. He had three times been charged with performing "illegal" operations, and in two cases, the female patients died. Twice he was acquitted, and the third case was dismissed on May 5, 1915, while Dr. Kellogg was treating Chris Evans for the circulatory problem.

Despite his legal difficulties, Dr. Kellogg had a large practice and a reputation as a brilliant surgeon. It is likely that Dr. Kellogg performed Evans's amputation at home and disposed of the amputated leg. Gruesome as it may sound, the patient could request burial of the body part. There was an area at Forestvale Cemetery set aside for this purpose, or the physician could incinerate the amputated limb. Whether Evans was involved in the decision and which disposal method Kellogg chose were considerations between the doctor and his patient or the patient's family.

By the evening of his surgery, Evans was resting comfortably in his own bed. As midnight approached, however, he took a sudden turn for the worse and died. Christmas Gift Evans was buried beneath a fine marble monument at Forestvale Cemetery next to his first wife and probably minus the leg he lost shortly before his death.

Evans's widow, Bertha Bellis Evans, lived on in the house and stayed active in her husband's business concerns, especially real estate. When her daughter, Margaret, married William D. Scott in 1921, the newlyweds made their home with Mrs. Evans. William worked as a machinist, Margaret was a stenographer and Bertha sold real estate. Bertha grew older and in February 1940, the eighty-three-year-old widow became ill and died suddenly in the home she had loved for more than forty years. She was buried next to her husband and his first wife.

Margaret Evans Scott and her brother, Lewis Evans of Amityville, New York, inherited the house. The Scotts, who had no children, remained in the family home. In 1977, Margaret passed away at the age of eighty in the house where she had been born. Lewis sold the house, and it passed out of the Evans family for the first time in nearly a century.

Margaret Evans, Chris Evans, Bertha Evans and Margaret Evans Scott all died in the house. Of the three, Chris might have the most pressing reason to come back for something he lost, but his may not be the only energy that manifests itself in the house.

According to a 1979 interview in the *Independent Record*, Nina and Eric Myhre had always admired the eye-catching home, and Nina was thrilled to discover that it was on the market. The Myhres bought the property. Ownership, however, proved a challenge. They discovered that the house had seen very few improvements since the late 1870s. Beautiful woodwork, original light fixtures and most of the original furniture were still in place, but the kitchen still had a wood cook stove. The Myhres replaced all the old wiring and plumbing, modernized the kitchen and poured a cement floor in the basement. They were kind to the house and loved it and its history. They even took the time to prepare a nomination and see the house added to the National Register of Historic Places in 1980.

In 1986, Mike and Dee Ann Cooney moved back to Helena from Washington, D.C., and needed temporary housing. The Myhres were headed to Arizona and offered them the house while Mike and Dee Ann looked for a permanent place. The arrangement was perfect. The Cooneys thoroughly enjoyed their stay in the historic home from November 1986 to April 1987. During that time, Dee Ann had two remarkable experiences.

Dee Ann recalled that they had settled into the Myhres' home when, late one evening, she was in the living room enjoying some quiet time. Mike and their son, Ryan, then a toddler, were already in bed upstairs. The house was very still and dark. Dee Ann sat in a small circle of light from a nearby lamp, reading. Out of the corner of her eye, she caught light or movement, which drew her eyes to the dark stairway. She saw an odd object about the size of a basketball, kind of misty, whitish and glowing. It was moving very slowly up the stairs.

Dee Ann vividly remembers that she felt no presence, nothing out of the ordinary. She was not at all frightened, just baffled. Although it was glowing, it didn't seem to cast any light around it. As she watched, the ball slowly ascended the stairs until it was out of sight. It was such a weird experience that Dee Ann didn't even react, and she didn't think to follow it. She almost thought that she was hallucinating. It was only in retrospect that she realized what a strange event she had witnessed.

Then it happened again. Dee Ann recalled the event with clarity and is fairly certain of the time sequence, that this was the second time. Again, Dee Ann was reading, and the house was very still. This time, she was sitting in a small room off the kitchen that they called the "piano room." She saw this three-dimensional ball of light hovering on the wall. As before, it moved very slowly. This time, though, it seemed to take a long time, and she stared at it for quite a while as it crept up the wall. She was more startled than before, and as it was happening, she remembered thinking how the ball looked exactly like the one from her previous experience. Finally, the glowing object moved through the ceiling and disappeared, presumably into the bedroom above. As before, Dee Ann was not afraid and didn't think to follow it upstairs.

The Cooneys found a house and moved before the Myhres returned from Arizona. The two couples did not cross paths and actually never met. Dee Ann thus had no opportunity to share her two memorable experiences with the homeowners.

The Myhres put the house on the market in 1990. The house was then vacant more than it was occupied, and the occasional residents never stayed long. Stories began to circulate. Denise King, a co-worker of mine at the Montana Historical Society, was house hunting in 1992, and the Evans house was on the market. She asked her realtor to show her the house. They pulled up in front, and the realtor handed Denise the key, saying that she would just wait in the car.

Denise let herself in and wandered through the downstairs. She noticed the antique furnishings, especially the beautiful dining room breakfront with gorgeous glass doors. As Denise moved to the back of the house, she distinctly heard what she thought was a cupboard door open and close, like the glass cupboard in the dining room breakfront. She thought the realtor had changed her mind and come in. Denise came back through the dining and living rooms. There was no sign of the realtor, so she started up the stairs. She got halfway up and stopped, thinking to herself, "Nope, this isn't where I want to be." She turned around and didn't look back.

Denise closed the front door behind her and headed to the car where the realtor was waiting. She thought about the cupboard opening and closing and asked her, "Did you change your mind and come in?"

"No way," said the realtor. "I won't go in that house. It's haunted."

A former colleague at the Montana Historical Society added an incident to the home's growing reputation. Her parents saw a garage sale at the house and stopped to look. A fine new swing set, installed in the backyard, was among the items for sale. They could not believe this find and wanted to buy it for their grandson. They asked the young couple why they were selling such a nice, new set. The young woman replied that they had lived in the house for several weeks and that they were moving out. "We just can't take it," she said. "We are afraid for the safety of our child." But she did not elaborate.

A legislator from Great Falls came to Helena for the 1995 session and needed a place to stay. Apartments and rooms are always hard to find when the legislators come to town. He rented a room in the Christmas Gift Evans House. It was a lovely room, with a bathroom down the hall. This was fine, for the owner was never there. He thought it would be ideal. He would have peace and quiet to work and could come and go as he pleased. He lasted three nights.

On the first night, the legislator was feeling very pleased to have found this great place. He locked up the house, left the bathroom light on since the surroundings were unfamiliar and went to bed. Not long after, he awoke with a start. The house was very dark. The only light filtered in from a pale winter moon. He felt a slight uneasiness at having awakened so abruptly and lay there trying to go back to sleep. As he drifted off, he heard a loud banging from somewhere downstairs. He dragged himself out of bed and felt his way in the dark, along the hallway to the bathroom. He fumbled around the corner to find the light switch. Hadn't he left that light on? He thought then that it might be a storm, and perhaps the lights had gone out. But no, the light came on cheerily. Someone, or something, had definitely turned it off.

Meanwhile, the banging continued downstairs. Maybe the cellar door had been left ajar and was banging in the wind. He turned on a few more lights and went downstairs to check, but the noise had stopped and there was no wind. Peering out, he could see the moonlight casting shadows around the yard. Everything seemed normal.

Morning came, the sun was shining and it seemed as if the whole thing was silly. Maybe the banging downstairs was just a dream. He headed out the door for a run. When he returned, he unlocked the door and stepped inside to the radio blaring upstairs. The radio had most definitely not been on when he left the house. What was going on?

That night the same thing happened again. He made his rounds, locked up, left the bathroom light on and turned in. Sometime later he suddenly awoke with his heart pounding. The rhythmic banging echoed in his ears. Again, he made his way down the hall to the bathroom to find the light he had left on turned off. The loud banging echoed up the stairway. As he listened, it seemed that maybe it came from the cellar, and maybe it was moving around the downstairs walls or around the foundation. Again he went down to investigate, but the banging stopped abruptly. The next morning when he returned from his jog tired and winded, he knew before he unlocked the door that again his radio would be blaring.

On his third night in the house, the same thing happened. He awakened with a start, but this time, he was full of dread. In a cold sweat, he listened to the familiar *bang, Bang, BANG!* But this time, he was too frightened to investigate, and the banging continued around the house all night. The next morning, the exhausted legislator packed his things and promised himself that he would never set foot in that house again. He had no knowledge of the home's history, nor did it occur to him that something was trying to attract his attention. Could this have been Christmas Gift Evans's way of showing his frustration over the loss of his leg and wondering about its whereabouts?

A few years later, another family had quite a different experience. The late Darlene Raundal called me in early 2004 to invite me to the Evans house. Darlene was an energetic, vivacious woman whose son, Garth Scott (no relation to William and Margaret Scott), was a single parent renting the Evans house. There was something Darlene wanted me to see. I was excited to see the house. At the appointed time, Darlene greeted me at the door and welcomed me into the home. The house was stunning. Tall ceilings, pristine dark woodwork and tall narrow windows transported me to a long-ago time. Some of the original furniture still graced the first-floor rooms.

Darlene ushered me into the dining room and gestured for me to sit down at the table. She explained that the family had gathered there a few weeks ago on Christmas Day. She said that there must have been thirty people around the table. Darlene spent much time preparing the meal, and it was a wonderful family dinner. They took lots of pictures. Darlene spread them out for me to see.

There were many photos of the family seated at the dinner table, from all different angles. Darlene selected a few.

"What do you see here?" she asked me. She pointed to a few shots that included the large breakfront behind the seated guests. This massive piece of furniture must have been original to the house. The cabinet doors—the same ones that Denise King thought she heard open and close—had gorgeous beveled glass.

Darlene again asked, "What do you see?" I looked at the photographs, and I could see a reflection in the glass. I said as much. Darlene asked me if I saw anyone at the table that resembled the reflection. This reflection was very distinctive. The person had a small goatee that came to a sharp point under his chin. It was a strange goatee on a stern-looking person. There was no one at the table who looked like that.

Darlene pulled a manila envelope from the breakfront and extracted a photo. "I found this envelope here," she said. "This is the National Register nomination for the Christmas Gift Evans House, and this," she continued as she handed me a photograph, "is Christmas Gift Evans."

A stern-looking man stared back at me. He had a distinctive goatee. It occurred to me that the photos with the reflection in the glass were taken on a day that was special to Chris Evans: Christmas Day was his birthday. Was this a coincidence or something else?

Darlene's son, Garth, came in, and we chatted for a moment about the photograph and the reflection in the glass. I asked him if his two kids were afraid at night. He said that his younger child was fearful at first but now felt good about living in the house. And thinking of the Great Falls legislator

Christmas Gift Evans was a stern-looking man with a distinctive goatee. *MHS Photograph Archives.*

and the banging at night, I asked if noises kept him awake. "Oh," he said. "No. I sleep with earplugs."

Almost ten years passed, and I added the Christmas Gift Evans stories to my Haunted Helena tours at Halloween. In 2012, as I started my tenth season with the Last Chance Tour Train trolley, Sonja was a new driver. As I talked her through the route, we paused at the Christmas Gift Evans House, and I told my stories. Suddenly she gasped.

"You're talking about my brother, Garth!" she burst out. I could hardly believe this coincidence. I had long wanted to interview Garth again and question him in detail about his time in the Evans house, but I had no idea how to contact him since his mother, Darlene, had passed away in 2010. I did not even know his last name.

So that is how I came to interview Garth Scott again after all that time. We sat down in November 2012, and I asked him about his impressions of the house. He told me that he was acquainted with the homeowner, who did not live in the house. The owner never made any comments about its reputation, but Garth heard plenty of stories from other friends. One friend who rented the house told him that he heard crashing and banging near the roof and thought for certain that the ghost was coming to get him. Then he discovered there were squirrels in the gutter.

The stories didn't bother Garth, and he moved into the house with his two kids in October 2003. He says it was wonderful for him and his family. The kids loved the house, and it was a very special time in their lives. His son was six, and his daughter was in high school. Garth recalled his daughter's prom, the fancy dinner he and his mom cooked for her and her friends and the memorable Christmas they celebrated there. Living in the house was a positive experience for all of them. They did hear noises, but he and the kids slept close together in the upstairs, and they never experienced anything negative.

Does Christmas Gift Evans's frustration over his missing limb explain the banging that terrified the Great Falls legislator? And did Evans soften his approach, showing his reflection in the glass on Christmas Day, the day of his birth? As a father himself, Chris Evans may have understood the importance of gentle haunting. But maybe the banging is symbolic of the turmoil the house has experienced. Not only did its walls witness the loss of a limb and four deaths, but perhaps the house felt Margaret Evans's and Margaret Scott's sorrow over the lack of children in their lives. These gentler spirits seem to have focused on the joy of having children in the house—the Cooneys' toddler and

Garth Scott's children brought new life into the home. Neither family experienced anything negative.

As Garth and I finished the interview, I asked him, "Do you believe the stories?"

His answer was this: "The house is very special. And let's just say it has something extra."

These varied experiences all point to one thing—there is some strong energy in the Christmas Gift Evans House. Its "something extra" is a gift that just seems to keep on giving.

Chapter 9

HAUNTED LANDSCAPES

The last twenty miles traveling into Helena from Missoula or Deer Lodge necessarily takes the modern wayfarer along U.S. Highway 12 over winding, scenic MacDonald Pass. This route over the Continental Divide at an elevation of 6,320 feet is one of Montana's many beautiful stretches of highway and affords some breathtaking panoramas of the Helena valley. The area is also steeped in history. It is a kind of pocket where many a traveler lost his way in the deep forests, fell victim to violence, froze to death or met with some other misfortune. The spirits of the lost, as some will attest, still traverse the rugged byway. Remnants of mining camps such as Marysville, Blackfoot City and Rimini dot the larger area where the ghosts of those who once worked the hills and made their homes in the tumbledown log buildings sigh into the wind; you can hear them if you listen.

Today, white crosses along Highway 12 speak to more recent tragedies in which traffic accidents have taken lives. There are a few stories—told when the sun sinks low and the evening chill sets in—that are especially memorable, that stick in the memory and become the stuff of disturbing dreams. The "Frenchwoman" who haunts the western slope of the pass is one that conjures such nightmares. Another is the episode of the lonely hitchhiker, reminding late-night travelers that when darkness falls, the pass may not be a comfortable place to travel. And on the eastern slope below the divide at nearby Rimini, hospitable former occupants, long dead, share their homes with current residents.

Ancient trails over the divide were known to generations of native people long before Reece Anderson and the Stuart brothers made the first recorded gold strike at Gold Creek in 1858. As prospectors discovered other golden veins east of the divide in 1864 at Last Chance and elsewhere, gold camps sprang up wherever there was a discovery. Within a few years, roads led from all points into the Helena valley. Mullan Pass and MacDonald Pass over the Continental Divide were two of the main arteries.

The Mullan Road, from Fort Benton, Montana, to Walla Walla, Washington, completed by Captain John Mullan in 1860, was Montana's first man-made transportation route. Arduously forged through wild and remote western Montana, it served as the first critical supply route to Montana's early mining camps. Freighters, prospectors and wagon trains traveled over Mullan Pass into Helena, and later in 1883, the Northern Pacific used this route to bring the first rail service over the Continental Divide. You can see occasional portions of the Mullan Road running parallel to U.S. 12 here and in other places in western Montana.

MacDonald Pass was born as part of a toll road in 1867, constructed by French would-be entrepreneur Constant Guyot. Unlike the Mullan Road, the toll road was well marked so that travelers could not lose their way in heavy snow, and at the toll gate, weary travelers and their worn-out livestock could find welcome food and lodging. A nineteenth-century narrative describes the old toll road at the pass as a gloomy, narrow thoroughfare through a forest of gigantic pines. The treetops arched over the path and shut out the sun, and the white limestone of the track was deeply worn and rutted. The precipitous pathway down the eastern slope was grueling and treacherous to wagons, animals and their human handlers.

Guyot had little to do with the road once he had constructed it. He left the collecting of tolls to his wife, who also ran a log tavern and hostelry commonly known as "the French Woman's." For a dollar, a traveler could get a good meal. Two dollars a night secured a space on the floor to put one's bedroll, a welcome prospect when the weather was inhospitable. With as many as thirty men spending the night on Madame Guyot's floor, she must have amassed quite a fortune in gold dust, the only currency of the early days. Madame reputedly kept her fortune hidden from her brutish husband, who had a reputation as a mean and abusive drunkard; he was his tavern's best customer.

On July 31, 1868, a Virginia City *Montana Post* reporter wrote of a journey to Blackfoot City, just west of Mullan Pass. He encountered the French woman at her hostelry and described her as the "garrulous, gossiping, good

A highway marker atop lonely MacDonald Pass tells the story of the Frenchwoman's Road. *Ellen Baumler*.

natured dispenser of ranch eggs and trout and tortured English." Several weeks later in August 1868, less than a year after the Guyots opened their toll road, passing travelers discovered Madame Guyot in a pool of blood, nearly decapitated from a bullet shot at close range into the back of her skull. Her property had been ransacked, and a fortune estimated at $6,000 in gold dust was missing. According to the *Post*, Madame Guyot had been saving her fortune so that she could return to France, where she had a highly accomplished daughter, in the fall.

Officials suspected Madame's husband, but no one was charged; the murder remains unsolved to this day. Local legend has it that Guyot left the territory and later was convicted of murdering his second wife. Before his execution for that crime, Guyot supposedly confessed to the murder of his first wife in Montana. But that story may be little more than an attempt to put the unsolved crime to rest. No one knows for sure.

There is no trace of Madame Guyot's log inn or her lonely grave, which long stood sentinel at the base of the western slope, overlooking what became known as the Frenchwoman's Road. But generations of locals believed that the Frenchwoman's spirit remained near the crumbling hostelry, terrifying travelers and guarding gold dust her murderer did not discover. Dr. C.S. Whitford, a Butte physician, is one who claims to have seen the Frenchwoman's ghost as he traveled over the old toll road between Deer Lodge and Helena in the fall of 1877.

As Dr. Whitford tells it, the night was miserably wet and stormy as he and his friend John Vial were making their way to Helena. They came upon the Frenchwoman's dilapidated hostelry and, thinking it abandoned, hoped to find some kind of shelter where they could camp. To their surprise, a proprietor appeared and, seeing the bedraggled travelers, beckoned them into the cabin while he took their worn-out horses to the stable. Inside the log house, they found a large room with a huge central fireplace in which a fire merrily crackled.

The proprietor soon returned and prepared a delicious supper, and then they lit their pipes and settled around the fire. The hour grew late, and the proprietor showed them to a small bedroom off the kitchen. It was usual for travelers to share a bed, and so the pair was quite satisfied to find a double bed and adequate furnishings. The two men prepared for the night, locked their door, pulled up the window shade to afford them a little moonlight and quickly settled into sleep.

Whitford awoke with a start and sat bolt upright in bed. A hazy figure stood in the moonlight. Whitford could see by the dim outline that it was female. She glided toward the bed, her arms outstretched. Whitford, panicked, tried to arouse his companion. He watched as the figure silently retreated to a corner of the room. Three times she gestured, as if beckoning Whitford to follow her. By the time Vial awakened, the figure was gone. Whitford told his friend what he had seen, but Vial had seen nothing and thus chalked up Whitford's blubbering to a vivid dream, turned over and promptly went back to sleep. Sleep would not come, however, to Whitford.

An hour or so passed as Whitford lay rigid with fear. To his horror, the ghastly apparition again appeared. This time, Whitford was wide awake. The room was deathly still but for the rhythmic breathing of Vial's deep sleep. The misty entity again stood in the corner, and as he watched her, Whitford aggressively shook his companion. When Vial finally awakened, Whitford described in detail all he saw as it was occurring, but again, Vial saw nothing. The woman came closer than she had before. She eerily beckoned with her right arm outstretched and then vanished as silently as she had appeared. Vial still saw nothing.

"Imagination!" he muttered groggily before turning over and going back to sleep.

Whitford lay frightened and wide awake. He decided to make Vial promise not to tell anyone about the night's strange events, lest acquaintances ridicule his story. Finally, when sunlight began to stream into the room and the oppressive darkness of night lifted, Whitford's eyelids became heavy. His fears vanished, and he fell into a restful sleep. Then again he awakened with a start. Daylight flooded the room, but that did not bother the Frenchwoman's ghost. She again stood tall in a filmy white shroud, her hair hanging in long tresses, her eyes deep, dark shadows.

Vial, now fully awake, could still see nothing and thought his friend had truly taken leave of his senses. The ghostly figure moved to the foot of the bed as Whitford's blood turned to ice. She silently moved to Vial's bedside, bent toward him and reached her arm over him to Whitford, who lay paralyzed on the other side of the bed. A scream stuck in Whitford's throat as he saw that she intended to touch him. With her icy outstretched fingers, the figure placed her deathly cold hand on Whitford's head. He could hardly breathe, the cold of her touch flowed through him like a river of ice. In that moment, he looked into the black depths of her eyes, and *she stared back*. Then, silent as the Grim Reaper, she disappeared.

For many decades, Whitford told no one. Then in 1927, two years before he put a gun to his head and ended his own life, the respected Butte physician told his story. Mulling over his frightful encounter of the Frenchwoman's ghost, he noted that when someone travels over lonely and deserted grounds where excited miners once trod, one travels over mysteries, dark secrets and bloody deeds carried out with only the hostile landscape as witness:

> *Hidden in some lonely nook many an unmarked and forgotten grave may yet be seen, within whose clammy, mildewed walls some unfortunate has slept these many years, and whose only crime was that of being near the murderous hand and heart that coveted his victim's gold.*

Remnants of the Frenchwoman's Road are still visible at the western base of the pass. Alexander MacDonald long managed the pass and purchased it in 1876. The pass was then named for him. In 1912, the county improved the pass with convict labor from the Montana State Prison at Deer Lodge. In 1927, MacDonald Pass became part of the new federal highway system. The primitive road was straightened, graded and graveled in the late 1920s and finally paved by 1935. In 1953, American Legion posts from towns across Montana began to place distinctive white metal crosses on the sites of fatal accidents along Montana's roadways. MacDonald Pass, considered a dangerous stretch of roadway, has always since had its crosses.

Most communities have at least one ghostly hitchhiker story, and MacDonald Pass is the perfect setting for such a tale. Similar generic urban legends have been told for centuries across the world and have found their way into most cities and towns. The vanishing hitchhiker has many variations and details that change to fit the location or situation. We have all heard tales like this, reminiscent of the 1965 song "Laurie" by Dickey Lee. MacDonald Pass and Helena have such a story, but this hitchhiker tale—unlike most—has a real measure of credibility.

A few years ago Buzz Helfert shared an experience that made quite an impression on him. He told me that when he was a kid, he loved to read the Sunday paper, and one of his favorite features was Al Gaskill's weekly column, "The Man in the Brown Derby," in the Helena *Independent Record*. Gaskill's insight into just about any topic was legendary, and the column was a community mainstay for decades.

As Gaskill neared the end of his life in 1973, he was a patient at Fort Harrison's V.A. Hospital. Buzz was serving in the 396th Station Hospital Army Reserve Unit as a medic. They did monthly drills at the V.A., and Buzz was thrilled to have Gaskill assigned to him as a patient. He told the veteran columnist how thrilling it was to meet him.

"Mr. Gaskill," he said as they shook hands, "I am such a fan of yours. I have read your columns since I was a little kid."

Gaskill thanked him and asked, "Do you have a favorite?"

Right away, he answered, "I sure do. I loved the one about the hitchhiker over MacDonald Pass. I read it over and over."

This particular column was a departure for Gaskill. In it, he recounted a very eerie late-night trip over MacDonald Pass. The driver, as Gaskill told it, was traveling from Missoula to Helena. It was very late when he passed through Elliston, the last town west of the divide. He was a little sleepy, and so he decided to stop at a pullout for a smoke before heading over the pass. The driver noticed that the American Legion had placed a white cross marking a traffic fatality at the edge of the pullout. The driver didn't dwell on it but rather took in the night air, admired the starry sky and drew deeply on his cigarette.

After a few minutes thus revived, he climbed back into his car. He started the ascent up the pass. Glancing in the rearview mirror, in the dim light he was taken aback to see a figure sitting in the back seat. He cranked his head around and saw that his passenger was a young lady. She was nicely dressed and rather nervously explained herself.

"I hope you don't mind," she said, "but I really need a ride into Helena tonight. I am meeting a friend at a dance at the Civic Center. Could you drop me there?"

Well, what could the driver do but agree to give the girl a lift? He figured she was from Elliston and felt that he should not leave her alone on the road. So he nodded to her and focused on his driving. The car, perfectly fine a moment before, began to pull to one side, and it was all he could do to keep it on the road.

"What the heck is going on?" he thought. "Do I have a flat tire?"

He was not about to stop on the road in the pitch dark. He made it over the pass, and as he negotiated the winding descent, the car returned to normal. He again glanced in the rearview mirror, and this time, he was confounded. The girl was not there; she had vanished without a trace.

The driver was badly shaken, and when he got to the west edge of Helena, he pulled into the Nite Owl Lounge for a stiff belt before heading home. He lay awake all night long thinking about the strange turn of events. He fretted and wondered where the girl had come from and how she could have disappeared like that.

The next day, he contacted a friend at the Department of Transportation and asked if he could discover the person commemorated by that white cross at the base of the west side of MacDonald Pass. The answer came later that day. A car full of teenagers headed to a dance at the Civic Center in Helena lost control. The accident took the life of one of the teens, a female.

The story has elements of the usual urban legend of the vanishing hitchhiker. However, according to Buzz, when he mentioned that this story was his favorite, Gaskill responded, "You know," he said, "I could have lost my job over that column. People would have called me crazy if I had written it the way it really happened. But I know that story is true," he said evenly, "because it happened to me."

Gaskill was a prolific writer, and a search of his columns—a very time-intensive exercise—has not brought this story to light. Buzz recalled reading it sometime around the early 1960s. I am certain that one of these days, when we least expect it, that column will surface.

The east side of MacDonald Pass, from the top of the divide down the mountainside, is still a steep and winding ten-minute drive into Helena. Midway, deep in the Helena National Forest, the former gold camp of Rimini nestles in the shadow of 8,800-foot Red Mountain. John Caplice discovered a rich vein in 1864, and a settlement grew around the claims. Territorial governor Schuyler Crosby named the gold camp in 1884. He had seen a production of the play *Francesca da Rimini* at Helena's Ming Opera House and suggested the name Rimini, pronounced "RIM-in-nee," after the Italian town of that name. But Irish miners assumed the name was Irish because Irishman Richard Barrett played the lead role. They changed the pronunciation to "RIM-in-eye," and it stuck.

Rimini boomed as the Northern Pacific Railroad's Rimini–Red Mountain branch line hauled gold, silver, lead and zinc ore to the smelter at East Helena. Local mines generated some $7 million. But the mines played out, and most moved on. The U.S. Army chose remote Rimini as its War Dog Reception and Training Center during World War II, where dogsled teams trained for search and rescue. A handful of residents today enjoy the solitude of the former camp, whose patchwork buildings and discarded mining equipment reflect varied time periods.

One family's experience at Rimini illustrates the spirited dynamics of some of these cast-off places and how special they can be to those attuned

The former mining camp of Rimini nestles in the shadow of Red Mountain. *Montana Photographs, 1896.*

to their ambience. Nancy, who prefers not to use her full name, wrote to me about her family's experiences and cherishes the time spent at Rimini. The family bought a former boardinghouse in 1984. Nancy wrote that it was a lively place for spirits, especially on Friday nights:

> *In the wee hours you would hear people going up and down the staircase, and doors opening and closing. It would become quite loud. They were wonderful ghosts, however. When I would ask them to quiet down because we were trying to sleep, the place would become silent.*

Nancy bought an old upright piano and brought it into the house. That night, she awakened to the sound of someone banging on the piano keys. She thought it was the kids, so she got up to check. The sound stopped the moment her foot hit the floor, and she found both children sound asleep. So she thought it must have been a dream, and she went back to bed. Again Nancy awakened, this time to the sound of a ragtime tune: "It was wonderful, if a bit creepy. My husband refused to go downstairs to check it out! I guess the prior residents were just so excited by the arrival of a piano that they couldn't resist. They never played it again."

The house had a very steep, narrow stairway, and Nancy worried that the children might fall. She spoke to the resident ghosts and asked them to help her keep an eye on the children. They did. Once, the youngest child started to tumble down the stairs but was suddenly stopped in midair and set upright. "You can believe," Nancy wrote, "that I thanked them profusely."

During their ten years at Rimini, the family also lived in a second house at which Nancy encountered pleasant spooks. It was a two-story log house that had been unoccupied for some thirty years. This house had an old gravity-fed water system, an outhouse and water rights grandfathered in to sustain one cow. The house had not been touched in many years, and Nancy faced a major challenge cleaning it out: "It was a wonderful house, very quiet, but once I bumped into a woman in an apron when I opened the pantry door. It was an odd feeling. I passed through her. Of course I apologized and said, 'Nice to meet you. I love your house,' and we both went about our business."

The house was completely furnished, left entirely intact as if the former residents would one day return. One resident apparently did return—or never left. Nancy had a friend who was visiting, and he sat down in the old rocking chair that had belonged to the previous owner. He came flying out of it and said, "I just sat on someone!" He freaked out while Nancy found it quite amusing.

The memories of Rimini are very special to Nancy, and she sums up her experiences by saying that it was a wonderful place to live. She notes that if you want to encounter its spirits, walk the street at 3:00 a.m. There, at the witching hour, you might meet a cluster of miners headed off to work their diggings. Nancy met them, and it was for her a most remarkable glimpse of Rimini's past.

Nearly a century separates the Frenchwoman and the hitchhiker. They are ghosts of different times, one of the dim long ago and the other of a more modern era. Yet these figures intertwine, sharing common threads: they are both tragic victims, and their stories endure, firmly entrenched in local lore. Complementing these two female spirits, the friendly residents of Rimini remind us that ghosts only require us to be receptive to their energy. For those who seek them out and for unsuspecting travelers passing through, these characters from the past make for spirited company.

Chapter 10

CAPTURED MOMENTS

Encounters with the shades that haunt our landscapes—on lonely mountaintops and passes, in windswept meadows, along rocky slopes, in abandoned places—compel us to think about those who were there before we were. Likewise, there are places in every town where many people have come and gone. Hotels, schools, offices, factories and churches are such places, and sometimes, when we spend time in these caches of energy, the past seems to intertwine with the present. Three places in Helena serve as ample illustrations: the first is a former industrial site, the second was a sanctuary for women and the third was a hospital. Today, all three of these places have modern uses unrelated to their original functions, but they all share rich histories, deep roots in Helena's early community and strong links to the past that seem to remain unbroken.

Just off Highway 12 on the western outskirts of Helena, the Stedman Foundry at 2668 Broadwater Avenue once manufactured everything from brass door keys to heavy mining and milling equipment. The single surviving building was originally Stedman's machine shop. Today, it houses Montana Fish, Wildlife and Parks' Montana Wild, a wildlife education center.

John Stedman located his foundry on the premises in 1892 after outgrowing several other locations. From 1892 until 1897, the foundry was a hub of activity where Stedman employed some fifty workers. On March 29, 1897, Stedman was enjoying a picnic with his wife when he suffered a fatal heart attack. The Stedman property then served numerous other businesses including a metal refinery; an assaying, ore testing and engineering business;

The Stedman Foundry, an industrial giant in the 1890s, is now Montana Fish, Wildlife and Parks' Montana Wild. *Chloe Katsilas, Rio de Luz Photography.*

and finally a gravel quarry operation. Helena Sand and Gravel's quarry pits behind the complex were later filled in to become Spring Meadow Lake, now a state park.

One day, Randi Triem and her son were following the trail around Spring Meadow Lake. Randi was pushing her daughter, Robin, in a stroller. Robin was born in China. Randi and her husband brought her home when the little girl was ten months old. Robin, now three, spoke well for her age but mostly in baby talk.

The three reached the site where the Stedman foundry had been. Robin unexpectedly pointed to it. In a clear and distinct voice, she said, "I used to work there."

Randi said, "WHAT?"

She repeated, "I used to work there."

Randi realized this was a unique moment, so she didn't want to prompt her too much. She asked, "Were you a man or a woman?"

"A woman."

"Did you speak English or Chinese?" Randi asked.

"Chinese."

Randi tried to ask her if she remembered anything else. But Robin changed the subject, and the moment was over. The hair on Randi's arms stood up. It remains unknown if any Chinese women worked at the site.

Industrial activity most certainly left impressions on the landscape and in Stedman's buildings. While the pattern house and foundry building were both destroyed by fire some years ago, the machine shop survives. Its thick stone walls are atypical; industrial buildings of the period were usually brick. An infrastructure of heavy wooden beams and steel I-beams, a lofty ceiling and tall windows distinguish the cavernous interior space. Massive timbers running the building's length accommodated a traveling crane or hoisting mechanism.

In 2011, the staff of six had not been settled long in the building when they began to notice some odd things. Education program assistant Patti Buckingham had the skulls of a dog and a wolf she used for teaching comparisons. She kept them along the stairs out of reach. It seemed that they often changed positions and locations. She thought maybe someone was moving them, but no one took responsibility. Supervisor Thomas Baumeister noticed something, too. He would come into his office to find pictures on his wall slightly tilted. Weird, he thought. And lights left off would sometimes turn on or vice versa.

One evening Patti was working late in her office on the mezzanine. She heard voices downstairs and figured there was an evening meeting in the auditorium. She skirted the area so as not to disrupt them, but when she came out into the parking lot, hers was the only car there. No one else was in the building. On another occasion, education program manager Laurie Evarts was sitting near the door to the auditorium during an evening meeting. Forty to fifty people were present. Laurie heard someone talking loudly outside the door and got up to see who it was, but no one was there.

When Patti heard the voices a second time, others in the office began to mention them, too. Some employees have also noticed fleeting shadows, reflections in the windows and wisps of smoke that catch the corner of the eye and then disappear. But the voices are the main attraction. Most everyone has heard them at one time or another. All agree they seem to be masculine, a kind of murmuring rise and fall, just low enough that you can't make out the words. They have tried to attribute the voices to the wind or to water running through the pipes. But those explanations don't make sense. The building's industrial character seems to blend with the voices—presumably of the men who once worked there. That the machine shop has plenty of energy packed away in its heavy stone walls best explains the phenomenon. It is not scary, or menacing, it just *is*.

In central Helena, a very different kind of facility occupies a corner in a quiet neighborhood. To most, it is a curiosity. A lovely Second Empire–

style house with a modest brick church tacked onto the back wraps around Ninth Avenue and Hoback Street. Next door, at 446 N. Hoback, a two-story barn-like frame building historically served as a dormitory, a purpose the casual passerby would never guess. The complex was originally the House of the Good Shepherd, where women and children in crisis could find a safe haven.

Bishop John Brondel, concerned about the immorality of Montana's wild mining camps, invited a small colony of the Sisters of the Good Shepherd from St. Paul, Minnesota, to Helena to establish a home for troubled girls and women. Five nuns arrived in 1889. The complex at the corner of Hoback and Ninth included a convent, sisters' chapel, dormitory and small church across Hoback Street. Multiple additions enlarged the dormitory, which also served as a school for the younger residents. By 1900, nine sisters cared for twenty-seven women and girls between the ages of eight and thirty-six. The older "inmates"—as they were called—operated a commercial laundry business in the dormitory basement that provided income for the home.

The House of the Good Shepherd offered sanctuary to women and girls. *Ellen Baumler.*

The sisters moved to the west edge of town in 1909, and their former convent is now apartments. For decades, the dormitory functioned as a furniture warehouse. In 1990, artist Tim Holmes began rehabilitation of the Hoback Street dormitory, converting the sprawling frame building to a studio. Tim enjoys the ambience of the rather odd space and has spent much time contemplating who lived there and what life might have been like for the girls and women under its roof. He suspects it was not always pleasant. For one thing, working conditions in the dim basement where the women did laundry could not have been good. Further, the girls and women were in desperate straits, with issues of addiction and abuse. One can only imagine children—referred by family members or the early legal system—confined there among adults with serious problems. Such a history of raw humanity and anguish bottled up within the space makes the present quite interesting.

As an artist, Tim is a sensitive person and aware of the building's strong ethos. He came to understand it through firsthand experiences—little things that seemed to add up. A few days after he moved in, Tim was heading up the narrow stairs at the back of the building. Midway up, the sickly sweet odor of decay hit him. He thought he would discover the corpse of a cat or some animal at the top of the stairs. Inexplicably, the terrible odor seemed to hover around one middle tread. To either side, up or down, the air was fine. He wondered how the awful odor could be so localized. He never found anything dead. Localization of an odor like that could have been a fluke, carried on some breeze (although there wasn't any) or paranormal, something left over from the past.

A year later, Tim had friends helping him do some construction in the building. At the end of the day, Tim would drop his tool belt and head home. He began to notice that sometimes when he gathered his tools the next morning, his tape measure would be missing. He would buy another, but he would always find the lost one in some strange place. He thought one of his friends was playing tricks. But then he let his friends go when he ran out of money, and it still happened. It happened so often that Tim began to document it in his journal. The last time he lost the tape measure, he got a call from a neighbor. She told him that there was a tape measure outside sitting on his trashcan. Sure enough, it was his. Then it didn't happen anymore.

Tim had a tenant living in the building for a while, and his sister also lived there for a period of time. The tenant saw a pan fly across the room. Tim's sister had a pencil holder full of pencils sitting on a table. She saw one pencil fly out of the holder and land on the other side of the room.

Then another series of incidents began. There was a small, first-floor room that Tim used as an office. Historically, it might have been the matron's bedroom. Tim often listens to music with headphones, and so it took some time for him to notice that if he sat quietly in his office, every so often, he could hear a short little female cry. Kind of like an "ooooh!" He felt sure it was a young girl, but he could never tell exactly where it came from or what emotion was behind it—surprise, joy, anger, fear or pain. It happened frequently, several times every hour, and only in the office. It was so regular that he got to the point where he could stop what he was doing and wait for it. He always heard it, as if on cue. When he hired a manager, he told her about it, and she could hear it too.

A few years ago, while Tim was away teaching a course in Washington, D.C., he called his manager, and as she sat in the office talking to him on the phone, Tim heard the cry over the phone. He told his manager, and she said she heard it, too. That was the last time. Tim went to Europe after that and was gone for a while. When he returned, he never heard the cry again.

Tim now lives in the building. One night, he was reading in bed very late. He heard footsteps in the room, about twelve feet away. Although he couldn't see them, he tracked the sound as it moved all the way across the room. Most recently, Tim was reading quietly in the living room. He heard a noise in the kitchen at the back. It was very subtle, like something lightweight had fallen, but it was also distinct. He went to investigate. A small piece of chocolate was on the floor, twelve feet from where he had put it.

Although the incidents have lessened in intensity, Tim is sure that long-ago energy lingers in the building. And it has yielded up some secret treasures over the years: plywood crosses wrapped in ribbon, a photograph nailed to a wall and covered over and, most poignant of all, a little girl's felt hat. The photograph and the hat now grace a wall in the studio where Tim pays respect to whomever they belonged. He understands the power of place the building holds, and the secrets it will never fully reveal.

Full-body apparitions are very rare, but there is one former institution in Helena where such a manifestation has occurred more than once. St. John's Building today houses diverse modern offices. The site on South Ewing Street dates back to the earliest community, however, when the Sisters of Charity of Leavenworth, Kansas, built St. Vincent's Academy for Girls in 1870. Earthquakes destroyed the academy and nearby St. John's Hospital in 1935. St. John's cornerstone was relaid with much fanfare in 1938, and the hospital rose again on the site of the academy. The sister administrators were iron willed and efficient, and their dedication was unswerving. In their long black robes, white caps and black veils, the Sisters of Charity were a familiar sight in Helena for more than a century.

Many of Helena's Catholic institutions closed in the 1960s; the hospital closed in 1973, but photographs of the sisters long continued to hang in the halls of the St. John's Building. Professional offices now occupy all four floors. The Rocky Mountain Care Center, a senior living facility, is attached at the south end. Those who have worked night shifts in the building tell eerie tales, especially about the elevator. When it travels the four floors of the former hospital, it sometimes carries a silent passenger. Many have seen her, and several employees have shared their experiences with me.

The encounters with the nun are essentially the same. The unsuspecting passenger enters the elevator, the doors close and only then does the passenger notice a figure standing in the back corner. She wears the distinctive habit of the Sisters of Charity: a flowing black robe and black veil over a white cap. The human passenger is inevitably frozen to the spot and exits quickly when the doors open. The sister stands motionless as the doors close. Those who have had this experience afterward opt for the stairway.

Bill Felton was a maintenance supervisor at the St. John's Building. Although now retired, he vividly recalls his own encounter with the nun. He heard all the stories about the elevator. It wasn't that he didn't believe the nun could be there, he just never gave it much thought—that is, until he met her, too. It was evening, around eight o'clock. Bill was on his way from the care center to St. John's, where he had to check on an employee. He entered St. John's from the south care center entrance. He walked down the hall toward the entry foyer, where the hospital admittance desk used to be.

Bill saw her standing in the foyer. In his mind's eye, he pictured the admittance desk with the nun there as it had been in 1960, and it didn't register that she was out of place. He recognized the habit of the Sisters of Charity, as he was familiar with the portraits that used to hang in building. He knew what their distinctive headgear looked like, and he took stock of the black robe and veil with the white band across the front. It didn't seem odd at first. Bill thought the nun must be visiting the nurse who had an office off the foyer. So he didn't miss a step and continued down the long hallway. As he got closer, he got to thinking about it; this was kind of odd, seeing a nun there. And as he got closer still, maybe twelve feet or so away, she turned her head slightly toward him. Then she disappeared. Only in retrospect did Bill realize that he had seen something extraordinary.

A foundry, a women's refuge and a hospital might seem to have little in common. But as the years roll by and the histories of these places evolve and their functions change, their links to the past remain constant. These links form an endless circle that every so often loops back to the beginning. Not all are aware of the power of place and its ability to re-create sensory perceptions through stored, or residual, energy. But for those who can experience it and understand its nuances, the past is a valuable tool toward a better appreciation of the present.

ABOUT THE AUTHOR

Ellen Baumler received her PhD in English, history and classics from the University of Kansas, where she was a fourth-generation Jayhawk. She has been the interpretive historian at the Montana Historical Society in Helena, Montana, since 1992. She is a teacher and an extraordinary tour guide, and she is passionate about sharing Montana's lesser-known history. A longtime member of the Humanities Montana Speakers Bureau, Baumler's expert storytelling has delighted audiences of all ages and interests across the state. She is a 2011 recipient of the Governor's Award for the Humanities and an award-winning author of many books and articles on diverse topics. She is best known for her spine-tingling, well-researched stories of Montana's haunted places.